BOUNCING BACK

by Gail Young

||SAMUEL FRENCH||

samuelfrench.co.uk

ISBN 978-0-573-11422-9

www.samuelfrench.co.uk

www.samuelfrench.com

FOR AMATEUR
PRODUCTION ENQUIRIES

UNITED KINGDOM AND WORLD
EXCLUDING NORTH AMERICA
plays@SamuelFrench-London.co.uk
020 7255 4302/01

UNITED STATES AND CANADA
info@SamuelFrench.com
1-866-598-8449

Each title is subject to availability from Samuel French,
depending upon country of performance.

THINKING ABOUT PERFORMING A SHOW?

There are thousands of plays and musicals available to perform from Samuel French right now, and applying for a licence is easier and more affordable than you might think

From classic plays to brand new musicals, from monologues to epic dramas, there are shows for everyone.

Plays and musicals are protected by copyright law so if you want to perform them, the first thing you'll need is a licence. This simple process helps support the playwright by ensuring they get paid for their work, and means that you'll have the documents you need to stage the show in public.

Not all our shows are available to perform all the time, so it's important to check and apply for a licence before you start rehearsals or commit to doing the show.

LEARN MORE & FIND THOUSANDS OF SHOWS

Browse our full range of plays and musicals and find out more about how to license a show

www.samuelfrench.co.uk/perform

Talk to the friendly experts in our Licensing team for advice on choosing a show, and help with licensing

plays@samuelfrench.co.uk   020 7387 9373

Acting Editions

BORN TO PERFORM

Playscripts designed from the ground up to work the way you do in rehearsal, performance and study

---

Larger, clearer text for easier reading

Wider margins for notes

Performance features such as character and props lists, sound and lighting cues, and more

---

+ CHOOSE A SIZE AND STYLE TO SUIT YOU

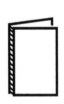

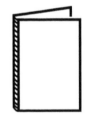

STANDARD EDITION

Our regular paperback book at our regular size

SPIRAL-BOUND EDITION

The same size as the Standard Edition, but with a sturdy, easy-to-fold, easy-to-hold spiral-bound spine

LARGE EDITION

A4 size and spiral bound, with larger text and a blank page for notes opposite every page of text. Perfect for technical and directing use

---

| LEARN MORE | samuelfrench.co.uk/actingeditions |

ABOUT THE AUTHOR

Gail has directed and acted with community theatre groups for many years in the Chester and Wirral area of north-west England. She turned her hand to writing in 2005, and took her first full-length play *Cheshire Cats* to the Edinburgh Fringe in 2006 with Guilden Sutton Players. The production was a 'Fringe Sell-Out Show 2006', was published by Samuel French in 2011, and has subsequently been performed worldwide, translated into other languages, and toured abroad.

Her second full-length play *Bothered and Bewildered* was a sell out at the Forum Studio Theatre in October 2014 with Tip Top Productions, was published by Samuel French in the spring of 2015, and is currently being performed up and down the UK and abroad.

Her latest full-length play, *Bouncing Back*, premiered at The Forum Studio Theatre in June 2016 to enthusiastic full houses, and focuses on the world of women returners to the sport of netball. All three plays are full-length comedy dramas with a social conscience, and focus on problems and issues that face women, families and friends in modern times.

See www.gailyoungplaywright.com for more information on all of Gail's work.

AUTHOR'S NOTE

I have always wanted to write a play about sport. I've seen many productions over the years that have focused on this subject and I've always found them uplifting. Having played in various school netball teams as goal defence, and being an older sister to both a PE teacher and a netball coach, there was only ever going to be one game that I would put pen to paper about. Netball, netball and netball. The Olympics may scorn it and view it as not worthy of a place on that particular world stage but we girls know better don't we? The truth of the matter is that this sport is enjoying a massive rise in popularity, with women of all ages and from all walks of life running (albeit some slower than others !) back to their local netball courts to join in the fun. Even better – the Netball World Cup is coming to Liverpool in 2019! So what better sport to celebrate?

I had an absolute blast doing the research for *Bouncing Back*, and a huge heartfelt thank you goes from me to the Golborne Back 2 Netball initiative which is run under the watchful eyes of their chairwoman, committee, and coach. They and all the team members made me feel so welcome at training sessions, league matches and social events, and happily put up with me wandering around with a pad and a pen eavesdropping on all the team talks (amongst other things...). You're all stars, and I couldn't have written it without you.

**Other plays by GAIL YOUNG
published by Samuel French**

Bothered and Bewildered

Cheshire Cats

FIND PERFECT PLAYS TO PERFORM AT
www.samuelfrench.co.uk

Bouncing Back premiered as a Gail Young Production at The Forum Studio Theatre in Chester in June 2016 with the following cast and crew:

CHARACTER	CAST MEMBER
ANGIE TASKER	Molly Clarke
ANNA BELL	Emma Careless
ASBO	Fiona MacSween
COUNCILLOR DRAKE	Mike Heathcote
JACKIE GOODWIN	Eileen Reisin
JANET WATSON	Vicki Daniels
KATH MAXWELL	Kat Wilson
MICKY OWENS	Joanne Sartorius
PHOTOGRAPHER	Luke Disley
ROB EVANS	Neil Mason
SARAH MORRIS	Theresa Bennett
TINA ROGERS	Emma Hind
TRACEY NEVILLE	Tracy Neville (who kindly recorded her lines for the show!)
TRISHA WILSON	Rachel Sumner
DJ	Luke Disley
MASCOT	Neil Mason

CREW

Co-Directors	Gail Young and Phil Cross
Choreography	Phil Cross
Producer	Brian Fray
Lighting Design	Phil Cross
DSM	Abbie Taylor
Video Operative	Abbie Taylor
Sound Design	Brian Fray
Lighting Operative	Josie McHugh

Special thanks from Gail Young go to Phil Cross for his inventive lighting design and choreography for the training and match sequences, and to Brian Fray for an absolutely brilliant soundscape. Thanks guys xx

See the following for production shots of the premiere of *Bouncing Back*
www.gailyoungplaywright.com
www.facebook.com/BouncingBackGailYoung

This play is dedicated to women returners to sport.
May they live long and prosper.

CHARACTER PROFILES

Trisha Wilson   Coach   40s
Trisha is a self- employed netball coach. Her husband passed
away a couple of years ago, and she is struggling to juggle work
and money/ being a single mum to her teenage daughter. Strong
character with a hard exterior and soft interior. Passionate about
the sport and her role in developing women returners to netball.

Rob Evans   Caretaker   40s
Confirmed bachelor. Meets Trisha who reminds him a lot of his
mum (who was also a single mother). He is the caretaker/manager
of the local run-down sports hall, initially sceptical about how the
Back 2 Netball initiative is going to work out... Will the girls win
him round? First love is football...

Kath Maxwell   Netballer GA   30s
GA – goal attack. Big mates with Janet (they are old school
friends). Has been dragged to the initial training session by Janet
as they both played netball at school. Lacks confidence at first but
rediscovers her love for the game.

Janet Watson   Netballer WD   early 30s
WD – wing defence. Janet – old school pal with Kath. Works in a
bank and thinking of starting a netball team at work. Persuades
Kath to come along to the Back 2 Netball sessions with her.

ASBO   Netballer GS   Playing age 30–40
GS – goal shooter. ASBO – the nickname says it all. Single.
Competitive. Has issues. She is an ex-soldier who is suffering from
post traumatic stress disorder but has refused counselling. Has a
drink problem.

Anna Bell   Netballer GD   Playing age early 30s
GD – goal defence. A born organiser. She has secured the funding
to start the Back 2 Netball training sessions and hired Trisha to
coach the group. Mum of young twins and wife of the needy John.
The rock of the team and a natural choice for team captain.

Micky Owens   Netballer WA   early 40s
WA – wing attack. The glamour girl of the team. In denial about the aging process and in love with her nails. Has a young daughter and a hubby who wants her to stay as fit and trim as possible.

Angie Tasker   Netballer sub   20
Super sub. Angie has taken a year out from university as she has been ill with glandular fever. Now at home with Mum and Dad and recovering. Youngest member of the squad but wiser than her years. Attends the training sessions with the encouragement of her next-door neighbour Sarah.

Sarah Morris   Netballer C   late 30s
C – centre. A nurse. Working mum. Fit, with loads of energy which is why she is made the centre in the team. Caring individual. Revisiting the game she loves.

Jackie Goodwin   Netballer sub   mid 40s
Substitute. Overweight. Mother of teenagers. Lacking self-confidence. But absolutely loves the game of netball and hero worships Tracey Neville – the England coach – and Manchester Thunder. Desperate to get fit, lose weight and be part of the team.

Tina Rogers   Netballer GK   30s
GK – goal keeper. Divorced. Calls a spade a spade. Sister-in-law to Anna which is how she found out about the Back 2 Netball training sessions. Needs to get out there after her divorce and focus on other things.

Councillor Drake   Male   40–60
Minor role but very important in the final scene of Act I. Slightly pompous local councillor who loves all the attention he receives from the netball players at the photo shoot for the local press.

Photographer   Male   20s–30s
Local photographer in Act I organising a rowdy and excited netball squad for their first photo shoot in their new team strip for the local press. Bit of a jack-the-lad type. Will double up as the DJ in the Manchester Thunder scene at the end of Act II.

Mascot: Can double up with the actors playing either Councillor Drake or Rob Evans.

ACT I

Scene One

A run-down sports hall in the north-west of England. Wooden floors, various pitch markings on the floor, very bare. At one end is a large untidy notice board with too many posters on it all fighting for attention.

ROB, the centre caretaker/manager enters. He is athletic-looking, wearing sports gear. He takes down out of date posters from the notice board and places a new notice on it, standing back to read it aloud.

ROB *(reading aloud)* "The Veterans Challenge Football Tournament. 14th June. Sixteen Teams blah blah blah... It is estimated that over 300 people will take part *(aside)* We live in hope! ...Councillor Drake will be presenting trophies on the day *(aside)* He'd do anything for a bloody photo opportunity. If you want to be part of this event or attend the regular football coaching session for veterans throughout the year contact our reception desk"... That should rake in a few pennies...

ROB decides the football notice is not prominent enough. He checks out a zumba notice that is already on the board.

Zumba...

ROB takes the zumba notice down from its very prominent position and places the football notice there. The zumba notice is shoved to a less central place on the board. He looks at another notice that he has in his hand.

Netball...

Laughs to himself. Finds a space on the outer margins of the board.

Puts the netball poster up haphazardly. Leaves the hall.

TRISHA, *the netball coach, enters dressed as a coach should be. She comes in and out with various pieces of training equipment and netballs. She starts to set the room up for the training session and her mobile phone goes off. While she is on the phone* ROB *enters.*

TRISHA *(on the phone)* Hello. Oh hi love...pie and chips...in the freezer... I've left some veg out – fresh – carrots and broccoli. Don't overboil them... Livvy... Livvy...are you listening...the pie is frozen so don't forget to read the heating instructions properly...yeah...yeah...back about ten. Make sure you get your homework done while I'm out too... OK ...see you later. *(She hangs up)*

ROB Do you think she'll live?

TRISHA Sorry? Oh – me daughter! Yeah yeah... She never reads the instructions on anything. Just says, "Well it looks cooked to me!" and bangs it on the plate.

ROB How old is she?

TRISHA Fourteen going on forty...

ROB My sisters used to drive me mum round the bloody bend when they were teenagers. Bet she gives you and her dad a few headaches...

TRISHA *(abruptly interrupting)* Her dad's dead.

Awkward pause. TRISHA *carries on putting the equipment out.*

ROB Sorry – I didn't mean to...

TRISHA *(interrupting)* Don't apologise. It was a while ago now...we're coping...she's coping...

TRISHA *checks her watch.*

The girls will be here soon so if you can open up those windows over there that'll be great thanks.

ROB Oh...right...right then...won't be a minute...

ROB *exits.* TRISHA *studies the notice board. Swaps the football poster and the netball posters on the board. She surveys her equipment, realises she has forgotten something.*

TRISHA Rope ladders...rope ladders... Christ! I've left them in the car.

TRISHA *rushes off.* ROB *re-enters.*

ROB I've done that... *(Realises* TRISHA *has left)* Oh...

He notices the repositioning that has gone on with the notice board. Laughs to himself.

The cheeky little mare...

ROB *busies himself swapping the football and netball posters on the board. As he does so* KATH *and* JANET *enter in training gear. They carry their bags and a bottle of water. Not sure of her surroundings,* KATH *approaches* ROB.

KATH Excuse me.

ROB Hello.

KATH Is this the right place for the netball coaching?

ROB *points at the netball net.*

Sorry – I didn't notice that.

ROB Better make that the first part of the training session then – how to recognise the nets!

He exits.

KATH Cheeky git! Who the bloody hell does he think he is!

JANET Oh don't take it so seriously – he was just having a laugh.

KATH I didn't want to come in the first place...

JANET Don't be so negative...

KATH I bloody hated netball at school.

JANET No you didn't.

KATH I did.

JANET You didn't – you just hated that PE teacher we had. Before that you were always in the school team...

KATH Yeah. Mrs Buxton. Bossy cow. Enough to put you off sport for life.

JANET Look – we're here now so let's enjoy it.

> **JANET** *picks up a netball that is with the coaching equipment and tosses it to* **KATH** *who drops her bottle of water to catch the netball.* **JANET** *laughs.*

There you go – you've still got it. Have a go at a shot – go on.

KATH Give over will you.

JANET Go on – you were a brilliant shot at school...

> **KATH** *approaches the net. She is just about to take the shot when* **TRISHA** *re-enters the room with the rope ladders.* **KATH** *quickly chucks the ball to* **JANET**.

TRISHA Hi. First to arrive? You two must be keen. Nice to meet you – my name's Trisha.

> *She shakes* **JANET**'s *hand.*

JANET I'm Janet Watson.

TRISHA Oh yeah – I remember talking to you on the phone when you enrolled. And this must be your friend, Kath?

KATH Yes – that's me.

TRISHA So...if I remember rightly you're a defender *(points to* **KATH***)* and you're a shooter *(points at* **JANET***)*

JANET *(laughs)* No – the other way round.

TRISHA Sorry. *(Points at* **JANET***)* Defender. *(Points at* **KATH***)* Shooter.

KATH Well – it was a long long time ago – I'm not sure how good I'll be now...

TRISHA Don't worry about it – you'll all be in the same boat tonight.

JANET What boat's that then?

TRISHA Women returners to netball.

As TRISHA *speaks the other women enter the hall (*ASBO, MICKY, TINA, ANGIE, SARAH, *and* JACKIE*) chatting to each other and putting their kit down on the hall floor.* ASBO *is ferociously chewing gum. She picks up a netball, bounces it very confidently and has a few shots at the net.* KATH *looks at* JANET.

KATH *(whispering)* Shit! She's big.

JANET ...solid...

KATH ...scary...

TRISHA *(claps her hands for attention from the women)* Hello ladies, hello. Lovely to see so many of you here – and on time too. I'm Trisha Wilson – I'll be your coach in the Back 2 Netball sessions. *(She checks her watch)* I should wait for Anna really seeing as she's organised this, but it's eight o'clock so we'd better get started...sit yourselves down on the benches *(the women sit on the wooden benches)* and I'll run through what you can expect from the training sessions.

ASBO Winning!

TRISHA Sorry?

ASBO Winning – that's what we want isn't it girls?

TRISHA Yes, well... I'm sure we all want that erm... *(Looks to* ASBO *for her name)*

ASBO ASBO

TRISHA ASBO?

ASBO Yeah... ASBO...

TRISHA ASBO? Is that your real... *(*ASBO *glares at her)* OK ...erm... ASBO...as I was saying...

ANNA *bursts into the hall.*

ANNA Soooo sorry I'm late everyone. Soooo so sorry Trisha. My twins have got that bloody virus that's going round.

TINA That tummy bug?

ANNA Yeah – so they're either fighting for the loo or throwing up at the moment.

TINA Too much information Anna...

ANNA Sorry Trisha. I meant to get here earlier to collect the subs and introduce you to everyone but I had to arrange for me mum to come and mind the kids coz John just can't cope when they're ill. He's never been good at nursing anyone – almost faints if he has to have a needle and he's even worse if anyone's throwing up so...

TINA *(interrupting)* Alright alright. We've all got the message. You're too soft with John – what you really mean is that he was planning on going out...

ANNA No, no Tina...it's the...

TINA Don't try and kid us, he's my little brother Anna – I know what he's like...

Awkward pause.

ASBO Aye aye – bit of a domestic!

The other girls giggle. TRISHA *takes up the slack.*

TRISHA No worries Anna. Just glad you're here. You can sort the subs out at the end of the session if that's ok?

ANNA *nods and sits on the bench with the others.* TRISHA *caries on with the meeting.*

Anna got in touch with me when she managed to secure a bit of funding from the council, so I think she deserves a round of applause for taking the initiative and making this all happen tonight.

Round of applause from the women. TRISHA *continues.*

Right. There's a few health and safety issues I need to check out. First of all – does anyone have any injuries or health issues that I need to be aware of?

Much shaking of heads, but SARAH *looks at* ANGIE, *who puts her hand up.*

Yes...? Sorry – I don't know all your names yet...

ANGIE Angie Tasker.

TRISHA Angie.

ANGIE I'm still recovering from...

SARAH She hasn't been too well lately.

TRISHA I'm sorry to hear that.

ANGIE I'm ok for the training but not for the games at the moment, I still get a bit tired – so is it alright for me to come to these sessions? I've cleared it with my doctor and he says I should be ok.

TRISHA Let's see how it all goes tonight Angie, and we'll agree how you progress from there. How's that?

ANGIE Thanks.

SARAH See! I told you it would be alright.

TRISHA Just listen to your body – I'm sure you'll be fine.

SARAH I'll look after you Angie – I'll block any bolshie buggers on the pitch!

TRISHA OK – moving on. Chewing gum...

ASBO *stops chewing. Pulls a "who me?" face. Some of the others start giggling at her.*

Not a good idea when you're participating in any sort of sport so if you can get rid of it now and make sure you don't bring any to future sessions please.

ASBO *removes the gum, walks over to the bin and dumps her gum.*

Thanks.

ASBO That's alright... Miss...

ASBO *curtsies and then re-joins the others on the bench.*

TRISHA Jewellery – you need to get rid of that – it's regarded as a weapon. So can you do that now. And tie your hair back next time please.

The girls take out earrings and any bracelets etc.

And last but not least – NAILS. Hold up the palms of your hands.

They all do so. TRISHA *walks up and down inspecting them.*

MICKY Nails?

TRISHA You'll get your hands checked by the referee in every game you play and if they are not short enough you'll be told to clip them back there and then. Looking at you lot some of you need to do that tonight when you get home.

KATH I've only had them done today.

TRISHA Well if you're serious you'll have to make some sacrifices won't you girls.

MICKY My Geoff won't like that at all. He pays for mine and they've cost a fortune.

TRISHA I'll be checking them at the next session so you've been warned. Right. We'll just do a bit of a round robin to introduce yourselves...starting with you Anna.

ANNA Me?

TRISHA Well stand up then. You're the one who's got the ball rolling on all of this.

ANNA Ok then. Anna Bell – and I LOVE netball. Last played about ten years ago before I had the twins – I spotted this opportunity for a bit of funding – and I just thought "Sod it" and I applied for it.

TINA And you got it!

ANNA Yep. I got it. And I got in touch with Trisha to coach us, and here we are.

TRISHA What do you want to get out of it all Anna.

ANNA What do I want? To play again – I love the game – and to get fit.

TINA *(interrupting)* And to be with her mates...

ANNA *sits down.*

TRISHA Go on...give us your name...

TINA Tina, I'm Anna's sister in law. Well, it's no secret – I split up with me husband last year – *(To the other girls)* He ran off with that old bitch from the bingo, Chrissy Clarke – do you know her? She's been desperate for a toyboy and the soft sod fell for it... Anyway, I just needed to get out there again – so Anna said come down to the netball with me – and here I am.

TRISHA When did you last play?

TINA I haven't played since I was at school – I left when I was sixteen.

TRISHA So that's...?

TINA Twenty years ago. Hard to believe isn't it? I don't look a day over 21...

TRISHA Thanks Tina. ASBO?

ASBO Christ...the bloody creeping death! Do I have to? *(Pause as* TRISHA *stares at her)* Ok then... I just want to do something competitive again – and maybe lose a bit of weight.

JACKIE Yeah – me too.

TRISHA And you are?

JACKIE Jackie Goodwin. I want to get fit but I can't stand going to the gym coz it's full of size 8 young women. I feel a right frump next to 'em all! Anyway, I've been watching the netball on Sky – that's what's got me interested in coming tonight. And I went to a Manchester Thunder League netball game the other week with some mates...

ANNA/ASBO/TINA *are really impressed.*

ASBO You lucky bugger. Bet that was brilliant.

JACKIE It was bloody fantastic.

ASBO I fancy going to see them as well.

ANNA Let's sort out a group outing...

MICKY The Thunder League? What's the Thunder League?

ASBO What's the Thunder League? Call yourself a netballer...

ANNA It's the netball version of the football Premier League.

TINA You know – all the top-class players play in it

JACKIE AND – did you know? In 2019 the Netball World Cup's coming to Liverpool!

Lights snap to a heavenly glow. We hear a harp. The NETBALLERS *all look up as one except for* TRISHA.

ALL The Netball World Cup. Ooooooh.

Lights snap back to the hall.

TRISHA There you go girls. You'll be in with a chance of playing in the World Cup if you train hard enough. You've got a few years to get yourselves fit enough for selection.

Laughing from the NETBALLERS.

ANNA Hey Jackie – was Tracy Neville there? She's amazing.

Lights snap to a heavenly glow. We hear a harp. The NETBALLERS *all look up as one. An image of* TRACY NEVILLE *is seen in the heavens.*

ALL Tracy Neville. Aaaaah. She's an angel.

Lights snap back to the hall.

JACKIE I looked and looked but I didn't see her. Tracey's the England coach now isn't she?

Lights snap back to the heavenly glow.

ALL *(softly chanting initially and building to a crescendo)*
Engerland... Engerland... Engerland... *(The* NETBALLERS
all jump up as though they are cheering the team on)
ENGERLAND...ENGERLAND...

Main lights snap back to the hall.

TRISHA Hello? Are we all still in the room?

JACKIE Sorry... I just get a bit carried away...

TRISHA Moving on *(looking at* SARAH*)* And you are?

SARAH Sarah Morris. I was the centre in the school team and
I loved it. That was years ago I know – and I'll probably be
rubbish now...but I'm going to have a go!

TRISHA Have you played since leaving school?

SARAH No, but I've tried to keep myself fit. You know...jogging
every other day and going to the gym when I can fit it in. My
only worry is that I'm a nurse so my shifts might interfere a
bit with the training...

TRISHA Don't worry too much about that...and you are? *(She
looks at* ANGIE*)*

ANGIE Angie. Sarah's one of our neighbours and she's told me
about tonight. I just hope I'm fit enough to keep up with
everyone else.

TRISHA I'm sure you'll be fine Angie. *(Looking at* KATH*)* How
about you?

Pause. KATH *is very nervous.*

KATH Me? Hello everybody... I'm Kath and I... God. I'm really
nervous talking in front of everyone...isn't that silly!

TRISHA Don't be. You're all new tonight. Go on...

KATH Well... Janet... *(She indicates her friend* JANET*)*

JANET That's me!

KATH Janet's a good pal of mine and she persuaded me to come
along. We used to play the game together at school, and I've
been a bit of a stay-at-home mum with the kids for the last

few years, bit mumsy – you know – so anyway – here I am and...

JANET Here WE are and I'm made up that Kath has come. I think we'll have a ball.

ASBO A netball!

Mock cheer from the others.

JANET Yeah, a "netball". I can't wait to get started. I'm thinking about starting up a netball team at work – at the bank – and thought I'd better get fit first and these sessions were advertised – so here I am!

TRISHA Thanks Janet. And that just leaves you. *(Indicates* **MICKY***)*

MICKY Just me! Little old me! I'm Micky, and... I'm...erm... thirty nine...

JANET On the way to the big four zero...

The others laugh.

MICKY *(talking over* **JANET***)* Like I was saying, my name's Micky Owens. I'm... thirty nine...I'm a mum. I've got a little girl, Lisa. She's ten and an absolute angel. I love her to bits.

TRISHA Thanks Micky...

MICKY *(talking over* **TRISHA***)* What else? Oh yes, I'm married to Geoff. He's a star – so attentive – and he suggested this for me as a keep fit exercise coz he knows I used to play in the team at school.

TRISHA OK, moving on...

MICKY *(carrying on)* Anyway, I work at the local opticians part time – Olivers – on the high street. Do you know it? Anyway, Geoff likes me to look as trim as possible. And he can be at home to look after Lisa the nights that the netball's on – so it all fits in really... Mind you, he's not going to be happy about the nails. Not at all. He does like me to look feminine. I mean, I do as well, and nice nails are all part of that aren't they? Still, it's a small sacrifice isn't it? Giving up a little bit of our femininity in the name of sport...

Momentary silence as they all stare at **MICKY**. **TRISHA**
moves the conversation on.

TRISHA Brilliant. Thanks everyone... Right – I'm going to set the
equipment up for a circuit session that will improve both
your overall fitness and netballing skills. After we've done
that we can have a little practise game, so get yourselves
ready while I'm setting things up...

TRISHA *busies herself setting up the circuit. Rope ladders
on the floor, skipping rope in one corner, mini hurdles
set up, small flat discs set up on the floor a bit like
stepping stones. While she is doing this the women get a
drink, ditch their sweatshirts, tie their hair up. There is
a BING BONG loudspeaker announcement from* **ROB**...

ROB *(on the loudspeaker)* Would the owner of the old blue
Range Rover currently blocking the front entrance come
and move it to an actual car parking space. Thank you.

TRISHA *curses to herself, checks she has her car keys in
her trackie bottoms pocket and runs out.* **ANNA** *carries
on setting out the hurdles for* **TRISHA**. **ASBO** *picks up a
netball and tries some practise shots.* **SARAH** *picks up a
ball and she,* **JACKIE** *and* **ANGIE** *start passing the ball
around between themselves. Whilst this activity is going
on* **MICKY** *approaches* **KATH** *and* **JANET**.

MICKY Don't I know you two from school?

KATH School?

MICKY Yeah – St Bede's – I'm sure you two were there when I
was...

JANET I don't recall...

MICKY *(interrupting)* Yeah we were – we had the same PE
teacher, Mrs Buxton, remember? She used to take us for
netball training?

KATH I remember that grumpy cow alright – but I can't place
you... Micky?

MICKY I was a few years ahead of you two...me name's really Michelle – you'd know me as Michelle O'Rourke, me maiden name? Remember?

JANET Michelle O'Rourke?

KATH Really? Get away...

ANNA shouts over to MICKY.

ANNA Micky – give me a hand with this rope ladder, it's all tangled up.

MICKY Coming! *(To KATH and JANET)* See you...

MICKY runs over to ANNA. KATH and JANET observe her.

KATH Bloody Hell.

JANET Michelle O'Rourke. Who'd have thought it?

KATH Christ! She's lost weight. She was a right two-ton Tessie at school.

JANET She's lost those NHS glasses too.

KATH Contact lenses! Yeah – they make SUCH a difference.

JANET Not to mention the hair colour.

KATH Wonder what colour she really is underneath that blonde mane?

JANET Grey probably...or heading that way...

KATH Mmmmm. Mind you the colour suits her...

JANET And the teeth! Amazing...that brace paid off in the end...

KATH Do you think she's had Botox?

JANET I don't know about that but I know one thing for definite.

KATH What's that?

JANET She's not thirty nine...

They both giggle.

TRISHA rushes back into the sports hall.

TRISHA Sorry about that everyone. Thanks for setting things up Anna. Right then. I'll just talk you through the way this will work.

TRISHA *holds up the skipping rope.*

Skipping! Nice uncomplicated exercise that you can all do in your own back gardens as well. Great for overall fitness, balance, timing...

TRISHA *moves to the rope ladder.*

Sarah – you said you've kept fit so you've talked yourself into this. Come over here and we'll demonstrate how this works.

SARAH *joins* **TRISHA** *at the rope ladder. She is positioned side on at the edge of the rope ladder which is on the floor in a straight line.* **TRISHA** *picks up a netball.*

OK – you're going to step in and out of the steps on the rope ladder side on while you and I pass the netball back and forth to one another – small fast side steps. Let's try it.

TRISHA *and* **SARAH** *do a quick demo for the others.*

Have we all got that?

SARAH *is puffing and blowing a bit.*

You ok?

SARAH Just getting me puff back...

TRISHA Remember folks, little side steps – try and do it as fast as you can without injuring yourself. Sarah and Angie and ASBO can start with that exercise.

The others nod agreement to **TRISHA** *but look a bit unsure behind her back.*

Jackie and Janet and Anna can do the mini hurdles exercise to begin. You need to do this side on *(she demonstrates)* and then forward *(she demonstrates)* OK? Little fast steps again girls.

ANNA/JACKIE /JANET Fine.

TRISHA *(moving to the wobble boards to demonstrate)* And
if Mickey, Kath and Tina can work on these *(*TRISHA
demonstrates) to improve your balance that would be
brilliant. And when I give the command on the whistle it is
time for your group to move in a clockwise direction round
the hall.

ASBO *(aside)* "On the whistle!" Sounds like one man and his
dog...

The women all move as if to start the circuit. TRISHA
intervenes.

TRISHA BUT before we start all of that we need to warm up.
We'll kick off with a warm-up jog on the spot, so find
yourself a bit of individual space – and go!

TRISHA *blows her whistle. The girls jog and chat. They
grow more and more shattered as the exercises progress
till nearly at a standstill by the time they do the arm
exercises at the end of the scene.*

High knees.

The girls do the exercise.

And heel flicks. *(Whistle)*

*The girls do the exercise. Really puffing and blowing at
the end of it all.*

Now I want you to bend your knees and take tiny fast side
steps to one end then back again. *(Whistle)*

The girls do the exercise. It looks quite funny.

And again, the other way round – faster *(whistle)*

The girls do the exercise faster – looks even funnier.

Remember. Those little steps really make you strong on the
court. Last warm up exercise – bend your legs and hold and
leap like a frog go round in a circle. *(Whistle)*

The girls do the exercise – lots of frog noises and giggling.

Too much giggling there girls. Stand up – arm stretches while you walk around and then we'll start the circuit...

They all do arm stretches and walk around.

Let's crack on. Go at your own pace and have some fun as well as working hard. Start on the whistle.

TRISHA *blows a short sharp blast on her whistle – the girls rush to their respective places on the circuit, and get started on their exercise. Much noise and excitement as they get to grips with the first exercise on the circuit.* TINA *blows a short sharp blast on her whistle. Momentary blackout and the lights snap up on the* NETBALLERS *having moved round clockwise and on to the next stage of the circuit. This continues and becomes faster and faster until the netballers are frozen in the moment on some exercises and lights snap on and off at a manic pace. Lights then snap on and stay on to reveal the* NETBALLERS *all on the verge of collapse and* TRISHA *winding up the session.*

Well done girls. Did you enjoy that?

NETBALLERS *(exhausted) (various)* Yeah/Great/Shattered/ Thanks.

TRISHA Great. Same time next week then. Goodnight ladies.

The NETBALLERS *gather their stuff together and exit.*

ROB *enters as they leave. He is holding financial papers in his hand.* TRISHA *is busy packing away the training equipment. He approaches her.*

ROB Hiya. How did your first session go?

TRISHA Fine. *(Still packing away the training gear)*

ROB You've got your work cut out with those girls but I bet they've all been looking forward to...

TRISHA Look – I haven't got a lot of time Rob. I need to get home.

ROB Right. Yeah...anyway... I just needed to see you about this – the hire charges for the hall.

TRISHA What about them?

ROB It's about...

TRISHA *(interrupting)* We've paid up front for the thirteen weeks of the league haven't we?

ROB Yes, but what's happ...

TRISHA *(interrupting again)* Well if I've paid what do you need to see me for?

ROB I think there's been a misunderstanding about the...

TRISHA *(interrupting again)* Look – I got the hire monies from Anna along with the coaching fees and then I hired the hall to hold the sessions in – if you've got any issues about...

ROB *(interrupting)* Can I get a word in?

TRISHA Sorry?

ROB I appreciate that you're in a rush but you haven't let me finish a sentence yet!

TRISHA Sorry...

ROB Thank you. Anyway, as I was saying...

TRISHA's *mobile phone rings.*

TRISHA Excuse me. I'll have to take this... Hello. Hiya Livvy. No, I'm on my way home now. I should be there in about twenty minutes. No...don't worry about the dog. I'll walk her round the block when I get home. OK love – see you soon. Bye... Bye...

ROB Look, it can wait if you like.

TRISHA No, no...but just get to the point will you Rob.

ROB You've underpaid for the hire of the hall.

TRISHA Underpaid! By how much?

ROB One hundred and sixty pounds.

TRISHA WHAT?

ROB I think there's been a mistake and...

TRISHA I'll say there's been a bloody mistake! One hundred and sixty pounds more? You're joking aren't you?

ROB The hire charges for the hall have gone up recently –admin must have sent out the old hourly rates to you and Anna. I don't know why this has happened and...

TRISHA Neither do I. One hundred and sixty pounds? Those girls think they've paid the full amount for the thirteen-week period. I just haven't got that Rob...

ROB I'm really sorry about all of this.

TRISHA Not half as sorry as I am. I'll have to get the extra subs in and let you know when I've got it...anyway, I haven't got time to argue the toss now... Livvy's been on her own all night and...

ROB No, no. You're right, you get off to your daughter – that's the most important thing...

TRISHA I'm not happy about this Rob...

ROB Look, I'm sorry for the mix up but...

TRISHA *(abruptly interrupting)* Yeah yeah yeah...some other time...

She shoots out of the door. ROB *watches her go. Looks at the financial paperwork again and shakes his head. Picks up his mobile. Rings a number.*

ROB Mum? You ok? Good. No...no... I'm still at work. Do you need anything? I could pick up some milk from the garage on my way home and drop it off if you need any...but if you're ok...good. What was that? How's *my* day been? *(He looks at the paperwork in his hand and shakes his head)* Fine, fine... Listen, I'll pop round tomorrow and we can have a cup of tea and put the world to rights...yeah...yeah... love you too Mum. See you tomorrow.

ROB *hangs up. Looks at his paperwork again and heaves a sigh. He exits as the lights dim on the scene.*

Scene Two

The netball court a couple of weeks later. ANGIE *is on the court practicing her shooting skills.* ROB *enters to pin a football notice on the board. He places it centrally – moving the netball notice to the outer margins of the board – chatting to* ANGIE *as he does so.*

ROB Hiya.

ANGIE Hi.

ROB You're early aren't you?

ANGIE I know. Is that ok? I just wanted to get a bit of practise in before we start the training session.

ROB It's fine. You carry on.

He watches her have a shot at goal.

Is that your position then – shooter?

ANGIE Goal shooter, yeah, it is – well, I mean... I used to play goal attack but I'm not as fit as I used to be, so I'm trying to become more of a goal shooter.

ROB You know, I always think you need to be a bit like a sniper to get goals consistently – have that killer instinct. That's what it's like in football anyhow.

ANGIE I don't know about that. I've never thought of myself as having a killer instinct.

ROB But you're focused aren't you – I mean, you must have really concentrated on getting fit again...

ANGIE How did you know about that?

ROB Sarah mentioned it to me... I know her coz me mum attends a clinic she looks after. Hey – I hope you don't mind me saying...

ANGIE No, No. Don't be daft...

Pause. ANGIE *tries another shot.*

ROB Do you think you stand a better chance of getting in the team as a goal shooter?

ANGIE Maybe in a couple of months... I won't make the team straight away... I mean...the netball games are an hour long. I'd probably collapse! I've packed in uni for a bit because I've been so tired all the time...

ROB Have you had to pack in uni?

ANGIE For a while...just taken a year out...it's all been a bit of a shock to my system... Glandular fever's literally a pain in the neck!

She takes another practise shot.

ROB Hey – not everyone has to be on the pitch all the time to make a difference you know. Look at how many last-minute substitutions in football have turned the game around. It'll be the same for you.

ANGIE Do you think so?

ROB I know so. Get yourself on that subs bench and practise hard and you'll be part of that team faster than you think. Anyway, I'd better go – the veteran footballers are playing outside tonight...five-a-side. I have to keep an eye on them. They don't move very fast but they're all hooligans at heart!

ANGIE laughs. ROB goes to leave.

See you.

He exits as SARAH enters.

Hey up. Here's another early bird!

SARAH Hiya Rob. How's your mum?

ROB Oh...you know...getting there...

SARAH Recovering from a hip replacement is a long haul.

ROB You're right. You know me mum though – she'll bounce back, she always does...

SARAH Tell her I was asking after her.

ROB I will. See you Sarah.

SARAH See you Rob...

ROB exits. **SARAH** *turns to* **ANGIE.**

I'm sorry I couldn't pick you up tonight Angie, but I've had to come straight from work. Did your dad give you a lift down?

ANGIE I jogged down.

SARAH Angie!

ANGIE What?

SARAH That's four miles! If your mum and dad knew they'd go mad. You know you're not supposed to overdo things.

ANGIE Well I won't tell them if you don't.

SARAH I won't tell them, but just think on – the last thing you need is a relapse.

ANGIE Stop worrying! Can I cadge a lift home?

SARAH Course you can...come on then...chuck us the ball...

They chuck the ball backwards and forwards to each other.

TRISHA/ANNA *and* **ASBO** *enter carrying all the kit for the circuit session.* **ANNA** *and* **ASBO** *start putting the equipment out.*

ANNA Hi girls.

SARAH AND ANGIE Hiya.

TRISHA You're keen. How long have you been here?

ANGIE About half an hour. I'm just trying to get in a bit of extra practise...

ASBO bounces one of the netballs up to the net and has a shot. As she does so TRISHA surveys the notice board, and swaps round the netball notice and the football notice.

ASBO Hey – you're not after the goal shooter slot in the team are you?

ANGIE No. No... I'm just...

SARAH *(interrupting)* What if she is?

ANNA Leave her alone ASBO. You carry on putting in the practise Angie. You're getting better every session.

ASBO Alright, alright you two. I was only joking... Christ! Keep your hair on.

The other NETBALLERS *enter gossiping, put their bags and water bottles down, and some scrape their hair back into pony tails.*

TRISHA Hello ladies. Nice to see we're all on time tonight. If you can sit on the benches as quickly as possible.

The NETBALLERS *assemble themselves.*

Hands.

The NETBALLERS *all hold up their hands in the air with the palms facing* TRISHA *– a bit like well trained puppies.* TRISHA *marches up and down looking at them. Stops in front of* MICKY *and hands her the nail clippers.*

MICKY Aar ey. I asked her to do them really short...

TRISHA Not short enough. Get over to that bin and clip those nails back...

MICKY does so – the others shouting "Geoff won't like that". 'How much did he pay for those?' and laughing at her...

TRISHA stands by ASBO.

Gum.

ASBO I'm not...

TRISHA You are! Get it in the bin.

ASBO goes to the bin and gets rid of her gum.

MICKY re-joins the group while TRISHA is talking and trots up to her and shows her nails. TRISHA nods that they are ok and **MICKY** *sits down again after she hands the nail clippers back to* **TRISHA**.

Before we get started tonight Anna wants to run over some things relating to team strips and money, and then I need to let you know what the team selection is for your first league game this Thursday night.

Lot of excitement amongst the girls.

ANNA *stands to address them all.*

ANNA Right – I'm trying to make sure we get the kit in time for our first league game on Thursday night. We got funding from the council for the netball strips which is great. And it's in the council colours – red and white.

KATH That reminds me of our old school tie colours.

JANET Oh yeah! I remember now...

ANNA Anyway – the sweatshirts have been sponsored by a local company. Micky managed to persuade her employers to put in some money towards it all...

MICKY *(interrupting)* That's right – but we've had a bit of a hiccup, and they said they can't afford it now.

TINA But never fear – Tina's here!

ANNA Luckily Tina knows someone who's just starting off in business.

TINA Yeah. They're setting up shop on the high street – and they're really happy to get involved so long as we put their logo on the kit.

SARAH Great stuff.

JACKIE Well done you.

TINA They've emailed the logo to the sweatshirt suppliers like you asked Anna – all a bit last-minute I know but we'll have them back by Thursday...

ANNA Great coz we'll be having a bit of a photo call that night...

MICKY Photo call?

ASBO Calm down Micky. It's not Hello magazine...

TRISHA It's just a bit of PR in the local paper for the club and the council.

ANNA So we all need to be here an hour early, get into our kit and looking lovely – and then be ready for the photographer.

JACKIE Did they do them in my size Tina? The dresses?

TINA Stop fretting Jackie – course they do them in your size.

JACKIE I bet I'll look a right sight in it all.

TINA No you won't, you'll look lovely.

SARAH Hey come on Jackie, you're doing great – how much weight have you lost in the last couple of weeks?

JACKIE Half a stone.

TINA There you go then. And I've lost a couple of pounds as well – so staying off the booze and running around like headless chickens in here is starting to pay off!

ANGIE We'll all look like sports stars on the night!

MICKY *(getting her mobile out of her bag)* I'll have to make a hair appointment for Thursday afternoon...

KATHY *(to JANET)* Here we go.

JANET Well, those hair extensions don't look after themselves now do they...

MICKY What was that?

JANET Nothing, nothing...

TRISHA Bit of quiet please...

ANNA Don't forget that you all need to be in the main hall for seven thirty for the photos –

TRISHA And the game starts at eight pm. A busy busy night for everyone. Your first league game.

ANNA I think that's all from me – apart from...can you all make sure you've set up a direct debit for the subs...

TRISHA Yeah. The subs have gone up a bit folks so get that money in asap.

Mutterings of "already?" etc from the players.

Some sort of misunderstanding about the rates. It works out at just over another £1 a week from each of you. It's not a lot more but it's important you pay up soon. Is that all Anna?

ANNA Yep – that's it for now.

TRISHA OK. (**TRISHA** *walks over and picks up a clipboard and netball bibs from her bag – she has her back to the girls*) Team selection.

The **NETBALLERS** *stop chatting and you can hear a pin drop. As one they all move and crowd behind her. She doesn't notice them. She turns as she speaks.*

I don't want anyone...hey hey, move back a bit girls. Gimme a bit of space will you! *(They move back)* I don't want anyone getting upset if they don't get the position they want. I expect folk to work hard for selection so it's not a done deal every game.

Lots of nodding and murmurs from the girls. **TRISHA** *lays the bibs in a line on the floor.*

The good news is that whoever isn't in the team will definitely be on the subs bench, so you're all in with a chance of playing on the night. Working from attack to defence the team is as follows: goal shooter – ASBO.

ASBO *(punches the air)* Yess! *(She grabs the bib as will the others when chosen)*

TRISHA Remember ASBO – practise makes perfect. I'm after consistency.

ASBO You know me boss. Eyes on the prize...eyes on the prize.

TRISHA Moving on – goal attack is Kath.

KATH Oh my God! Oh my God. I'm welling up here...

JANET I told you you'd get it!

TRISHA I think you'll work well with ASBO – we'll focus on that tonight.

KATH You won't regret it Trisha.

TRISHA Wing attack – Micky Owens.

MICKY *(screams with delight)* Oh fantastic. Just brilliant! Oh I can't wait to tell Geoff and Lisa. Geoff won't believe it! He won't believe it!

TRISHA You deserve it – just keep those bloody nails trimmed back!

MICKY I will, I will.

TRISHA Centre...

> SARAH *has her eyes closed and her fingers crossed.*

TRISHA You can open your eyes Sarah coz it's you.

> SARAH *squeals.* ANGIE *gives her a hug.*

You're the right person for that position Sarah. If you were a cup of coffee you'd be an expresso! Now then...oh yes... Wing defence is... Janet.

> JANET *and* KATH *hug each other.*

JANET It's like we're back at school again Kath – me wing defence and you goal attack!

KATH I know, I know...

TRISHA Well done.

JANET I can't wait for Thursday night now...

TRISHA Goal defence – Anna.

ANNA *(modest)* Thanks Trisha.

ASBO *(shouts across)* Good one. You deserve that Anna.

TINA She does. *(*TINA *gives* ANNA *a hug)*

TRISHA We need a real leader in that position.

ANNA Thanks Trisha.

TRISHA I might as tell you all now that Anna will be the team captain on Thursday.

All congratulate **ANNA.**

Last but not least – goal keeper.

ANGIE, TINA *and* **JACKIE** *all look at* **TRISHA.**

It's Tina.

TINA Me? Really?

TRISHA Yes you.

ANGIE *(sincere)* Well done Tina.

JACKIE *(totally fed up)* Yeah – well done Tina. You've worked hard for that

TINA I'm gobsmacked.

TRISHA Well don't be – just play well on the night. Remember the motto for a good goalkeeper is...

ALL *(as in Lord of the Rings)* You shall not pass!

TRISHA That's right! You and Anna know each other so well you can almost read each other's minds.

ANGIE *and* **JACKIE** *look disappointed.* **TRISHA** *turns to them.*

Sorry girls. But you're the two subs so you're still in with a chance.

JACKIE *(miffed she has not been selected)* Whatever...you've got to pick the best... I suppose...

ANGIE Enjoy it everyone.

TRISHA *(to the team)* And don't forget that these two *(indicating* **ANGIE** *and* **JACKIE***)* will be itching to get into the team to replace anyone that isn't coming up with the goods on the night, won't you girls?

JACKIE Too bloody right we will.

ANGIE But we'll be doing a lot of cheering as well!

TRISHA That's the spirit – they'll need all the encouragement they can get...

ASBO Team name?

TRISHA Sorry?

ASBO Team name...what are we going to call ourselves?

MICKY Oh yeah.

They all have a think.

MICKY *(dressed in pink from head to foot)* How about "Pink Ladies"? I love pink!

JANET So we've noticed. What colour's the strip Anna?

ANNA Red and white – the council colours.

KATH Well "Pink Ladies" is out then.

ANGIE How about "The Red Perils"?

SARAH Nah. Sounds a bit like a disease... I have enough of that at work...

Momentary pause as they still try and think of names. **TINA** *jumps up and shushes the others to make her announcement.*

TINA Cunning Stunts?

ALL *(shocked but laughing)* Tina!

TINA Well – they wouldn't forget us with a name like that would they?

ANNA True!

ASBO Ball busters?

JACKIE Huh! If we end up playing rubbish...they'll think we're a balls up...

ASBO Tyronassballsup Rex?

They all laugh.

TRISHA You need to think of something you've all got in common... *(Her phone goes)* Scuse me. *(She answers it)* Hi

Livvy. You OK? *(Big sigh)* No...no. I'll take the dog for a walk when I get home...yeah...see you later... *(She hangs up)* Sorry about that.

ANGIE   What kind of a dog have you got Trisha? I love dogs.

TRISHA   She's a little terrier. Got a lot of attitude. A bit like you lot!

JACKIE   Hey – that's it. Trisha's Terriers! Let's call ourselves Trisha's Terriers!

All the others agree.

ANNA   Yeah – yeah. I like that Jackie. Hands up for Trisha's Terriers then?

They all put up their hands to agree.

TRISHA   *(laughing)* I'm honoured girls. Can't wait to get home and tell the dog!

ROB *enters the hall and looks across at* TRISHA *to indicate he needs to speak to her.*

(Checks her watch) OK ladies, if you can spend the next few minutes on the rope ladder exercise – I won't be a minute.

TRISHA *walks over to* ROB. *The netballers feign disinterest but are all eavesdropping.*

Yes?

ROB   Hi. I just wondered if you'd had a chance to sort out the hall hire fees?

TRISHA   Hire fees?

ROB   The underpayment. Remember? We had that conversation the other week and you said you would...

TRISHA   *(interrupting)* Yeah yeah yeah... I remember.

ROB   Well you didn't get back to me and I need to settle the account.

TRISHA Sorry...sorry about that. I've been a bit pushed for time. I should be able to sort it out by Thursday night. Are you around about six thirty?

ROB I'm here, and that's fine but it will have to be sorted soon.

TRISHA It will be – don't worry.

ROB Well, I'll let you get back to the training session.

TRISHA Thanks.

ROB And Trisha.

TRISHA Yes?

ROB Well done mate – I think you're doing a great job with them. A great job. See you.

ROB *exits.* TRISHA *watches him go. The netballers watch on.*

TRISHA *(quietly to herself)* Thanks Rob. *(Turns to face the* NETBALLERS. *Shouts)*

Come on then girls, line up for the warm-up exercises...

The NETBALLERS *all line up against the wall looking ready to sprint.*

TRISHA *blows the whistle.*

Blackout.

Scene Three

Spotlit scene. ROB *is on his mobile to his mum.*

ROB Alright Mum? Good, good. Has our Gemma been round tonight then? Great – yeah...yeah... So what are you up to tomorrow then... Listen – I'll drop round on my way to work tomorrow...no no...it's no bother. Get the kettle on at the usual time. Look after yourself...me too...see you tomorrow.

He hangs up and immediately rings another number.

Gemma? Hiya Sis. How was she tonight? I know... I know... she's as tough as old boots isn't she. That's half her problem... never complains...little steps but she's getting there isn't she. I'll whip round tomorrow on my way to work, do the milk run and have a cup of tea and put the world to rights with her. OK... See you Sis.

He hangs up. The lights fade on the scene.

Scene Four

Sudden spotlight on ASBO. *She is looking a bit rough and brushing her hair. She downs a glass of alcohol, chucking the empty bottle into a bin bag that contains other bottles. She is dressed ready to go to training. Smells her breath in her hands. Recoils.*

She takes a strip of chewing gum out of her pocket and starts to chew away. Smells her breath in her hands again. Picks up the clinking bin bag as well as her training bag. Exits.

Blackout.

Ding dong of a doorbell in the darkness. Spotlight comes up on JACKIE *and* SARAH *in* JACKIE's *hallway.*

SARAH Are you ready Jackie?

JACKIE Nearly. *(She is knelt stuffing things into her training bag)* Thanks for picking me up tonight. Where's Angie?

SARAH Waiting in the car.

JACKIE I've had to lend our Joe my car – he's taking his girlfriend out tonight – a special date he says!

SARAH Teenagers! They don't think you've got a life of your own do they?

JACKIE Who's minding your little one?

SARAH Me mum. Adam's on nights so getting out for this photo-shoot turned into a bit of a nightmare. Thank God me mum offered to mind the kids at the last minute.

JACKIE You're dead lucky – I wish I'd had that much support when mine were little. I wouldn't have so much weight to shift now.

SARAH Stop putting yourself down. You've really come on since you started the netball.

JACKIE I haven't lost a lot of weight yet. But my stamina is a lot better. I'm running now as well – two miles a day...

SARAH Get you!

JACKIE I feel fantastic when I'm done. And it's all down to netball! It's changing my life!

SARAH Never mind making our team, you'll make the Thunder League one day – you will!

JACKIE Aah – that'd be great wouldn't it?

> JACKIE *looks up and we hear a harp play.* JACKIE *is bathed in a heavenly spotlight. We hear* TRACY NEVILLE*'s voice softly echo the words, "Jackie Goodwin. What a player!! A future England star..."*

SARAH Jackie... Jackie... JACKIE!

> *The spotlight and harp snap off as* JACKIE *comes back to reality.*

Hey... Come on...we're going to be late if we don't get a move on.

JACKIE Sorry! All packed – let's go.

> *They exit and the spot cross fades to* KATH *and* JANET.

KATH You ready then?

> JANET *is on her mobile and holds up her hand to apologise to* KATH *as she finishes the call.*

JANET *(on her mobile)* Yes...yeah. I can't make Friday...how about Saturday? Eight o'clock. Yeah...that's fine... I'll meet you there then. See you... Bye... *(She hangs up)* Sorry Kath.

KATH Off out on Saturday?

JANET Yeh...with Shelley...

KATH Really... Shelley? You seeing her again then?

JANET Yeah.

KATH You need to be careful! I'm really anti internet dating. I'd be terrified of meeting a psycho...

JANET Gotta confess I have met a few nutters...but she seemed really nice on the first date...and I'm so bloody busy at work

I just haven't got time to get out there and meet people any other way.

KATH And now you've got to fit the netball in as well!

JANET Hey – the netball's worth it! It's a real stress buster for me after being in bloody meetings and staring at a computer screen all day!

KATH It's a stress buster for all of us. *(Beat)* Hey, have you thought any more about...

JANET interrupts.

JANET Letting the team know? Don't know how comfortable I'd be with coming out to them at the moment.

KATH Might be best sooner rather than later.

JANET Yeah... I know. But it took me long enough to tell you and you're one of me best mates!

KATH True!

JANET I'll think about it but it's not top of my list of priorities. Winning this game tonight is though!

KATH Come on then or we'll be late for the photo shoot.

They exit. Lights cross fade to ANNA and TINA who are outside the sports hall.

ANNA Have you got everything out of the car?

TINA Yep. Let's get in there. I can't wait to see the new kit on everyone!

ANNA's mobile rings and she looks at it and lets out a big sigh.

TINA Who is it?

ANNA John.

TINA Our John! What the hell does he want now?

ANNA God knows – he always wants something when I'm going to training.

ANNA goes to answer the phone and TINA snatches it off her and takes the call.

TINA   Hello – no, I know you haven't rung my number John, Anna's not available.

ANNA   Give it here will you.

TINA hangs on to the phone.

TINA   John – you knew she was going out tonight, so just get on with minding the kids will you. You're a big lad now – you're not my snotty nosed little brother any more. Grow up or I'll come round and smack your arse.

TINA ends the call. She looks at ANNA and they both start laughing.

Get your bullshit detector seen too Anna! You're too bloody soft with him! I can read him like a book...he always was an attention-seeking little so and so.

ANNA   I know... I know...

TINA   I'll be having Big Sister words with him tonight after training. Come on – it's our big night tonight!

She puts her arm round ANNA's shoulder as they both exit. The spot fades.

Scene Five

Lights come up on ROB *in the hall checking out the netball posts for the big night of the photo shoot. He tidies up the notice board. Moves the football notice to the middle of the board and the netball poster to the outer regions of the board. He checks his watch.* TRISHA *enters.*

ROB Hiya.

TRISHA Hi.

ROB Thanks for coming in a bit early to get this all sorted.

TRISHA No problem.

She hands him a cheque. He looks at it.

ROB One Hundred and Sixty.

TRISHA That's right – One Hundred and Sixty.

ROB I thought you needed time to get in the...

TRISHA *interrupts him.*

TRISHA Get in the subs? Yes I did – and they weren't happy about having to pay more! Anyway, you've got it now – I just needed a bit of breathing space...

ROB I see.

TRISHA Sorry I was a bit of a bitch about it all. Money's been a bit tight and I've had to juggle a few things... I just couldn't afford to pay it out till I got the cash in...

ROB Hey – don't apologise. We've all been there.

TRISHA Yeah, I suppose so.

She turns away from him.

ROB Trisha? Are you alright.

TRISHA I'm fine, I'm fine.

ROB No you're not. Can I do anything? Do you need me to wait on the money a bit longer?

TRISHA No, no... I was just waiting for the subs to come in from everyone...bit of a pain really...cash flow...chasing money all the time...goes with the job I suppose...and then Livvy needed some dosh for another school trip... It just all gets on top of me sometimes...

Pause as TRISHA *tries to gather herself together. She is in tears.*

ROB It's hard isn't it?

TRISHA What?

ROB Being on your own. My mum went through all of that.

TRISHA Did she? When did your dad pass away then Rob?

ROB Oh he isn't dead. He just buggered off when we were all little. I was the youngest.

TRISHA That must have been tough on you.

ROB Not really. I was only three so I didn't really know him. It was tough for me mum though...you remind me of her sometimes...

TRISHA Me?

ROB You're a grafter. You'll get through it all Trisha, like she did, I know you will.

TRISHA Hey – pack it in will you – I'll be blubbing again and that photographer will be here soon for the photo shoot. Do I look like I've been crying? Are my eyes all red?

ROB *walks up to her and looks into her eyes.*

ROB No. They're a beautiful shade of blue. Very striking...

Silence as they look at each other. Suddenly all the over-excited netballers (except MICKY *and* ANNA*) burst in wearing their brand new netball dresses. They are accompanied by loud music that* ASBO *is playing on her iphone –* "*VOGUE*" *by Madonna.*

ASBO HELLO magazine here we come!

She and the girls walk an imaginary catwalk showing off their team strip – striking vogue poses. ASBO *chews gum ferociously.*

JACKIE What do you think Trisha?

TRISHA You all look wonderful. Very professional.

ANNA rushes in carrying a bag with the team sweatshirts in which she dumps on the bench.

ANNA Councillor Drake is here, and the photographer. They're just doing a head shot of him outside before we have the team photos taken.

ANGIE Do you think we need any props Trisha?

TRISHA Props?

ANGIE You know, like netballs.

SARAH Don't be so daft.

TRISHA Well maybe just one. *(she throws ANGIE a netball)* There you go super sub. ASBO, come here.

ASBO *(walking up to TRISHA and striking a model pose)* What?

TRISHA Dump the chewing gum.

ASBO marches to the bin in a huff to dump the chewing gum.

JACKIE *(following ASBO)* Hey ASBO, I saw you in The Three Stags last night. Are you sober yet?

ASBO Shut up Jackie... I just hope me liver doesn't explode while I'm playing...

ANNA *(checking the door and shouting)* They're here, they're here...

The PHOTOGRAPHER and COUNCILLOR DRAKE appear.

ROB I'll leave you all to it then. Enjoy the night girls. See you Trisha.

TRISHA Yeah – see you Rob.

ROB *gives* TRISHA *a smile and exits,* JANET *and* KATH *sidle up to* TRISHA *and look on.*

JANET Oooooh! I think he's sweet on you Trisha.

KATH Bit of a romance brewing there Coach.

TRISHA Button it you two, and get over there with the others and butter up Councillor Drake...

JANET and KATH Yes boss!

COUNCILLOR DRAKE *is surrounded by* NETBALLERS *and loving every minute of it. The* NETBALLERS *are all singing* **"CHAMPIONS, CHAMPIONS"** *as they line up with him to have their picture taken.* TRISHA *looks on.* MICKY *rushes into the hall.* ANNA *follows her.*

ANNA Where the hell have you been?

ASBO *(shouts over)* Shaving her legs.

MICKY I haven't!

ASBO You have. I saw you with your leg in the sink and your razor in your hand...

ANNA That'll do. Get in the line-up Micky and smile sweetly for the camera.

MICKY *joins the line-up.*

PHOTOGRAPHER Right folks, all look at the camera. Stand side on. That's it, smile – don't blink...that's it. Well done.

ANNA *and the others shout over to* TRISHA *to get in on a shot.*

ANNA Hey come on Trisha. You need to be in on a picture as well. Get in here.

TRISHA *joins them all. Another photograph is taken.*

PHOTOGRAPHER And if you ladies can all put on your sweatshirts we can take another few shots of you showing the name of your other sponsors on your kit...

The NETBALLERS *all break ranks and mill around putting on their sweatshirts.* TRISHA *and* COUNCILLOR

DRAKE *move away from them chatting while the* NETBALLERS *put their sweatshirts and get ready for the next shot.*

COUNCILLOR DRAKE This is a wonderful sporting initiative for the women of the borough Trisha.

TRISHA You're right. It's really good of the council to invest some money in it.

COUNCILLOR DRAKE You've got Anna to thank for that. She's a very persuasive lady.

TRISHA A natural leader our Anna. That's why she's been appointed team captain.

COUNCILLOR DRAKE Well deserved I'm sure. Well deserved. Who are the sponsors for the rest of the kit then?

TRISHA Anna's sister-in-law Tina sorted it all out. A little local business on the high street – I think it's a pet grooming salon...

COUNCILLOR DRAKE Wonderful. Wonderful. It's good to see local businesses supporting these sort of things...

During the above conversation it is imperative that the NETBALLERS *don't reveal the logo on the back of their sweatshirts until the last possible second.*

PHOTOGRAPHER OK girls, we'll have one of all of you and the councillor facing the front first.

The COUNCILLOR *joins the* NETBALLERS *standing in the middle of the formation, The girls are all singing* **"CHAMPIONS CHAMPIONS"** *again...*

Right girls. A bit of hush please. Great, and...smile...perfect. If you could just go over there now Councillor Drake and stand out of shot with Trisha.

COUNCILLOR DRAKE Fine, fine...

The COUNCILLOR *goes and stands by* TRISHA. *They look on as the team photo is taken.*

PHOTOGRAPHER Now girls, on the count of three you're all going to stand with your back to me and then look over your left shoulder to the camera and smile.

MICKY Left shoulder? My right side is more photogenic really...

PHOTOGRAPHER Left shoulder...one...two...three...turn. *(they all turn as one)* Smile...*(they all look over their left shoulder)* ...smile... *(They all smile)*

The **NETBALLERS** *are all busy posing and smiling for the photographer.*

COUNCILLOR DRAKE *(whispering to* **TRISHA***)* Does that say what I think it says?

TRISHA Sorry?

COUNCILLOR DRAKE Unusual logo for a ladies team...

TRISHA *(trying not to laugh)* Well, the sponsor is a pet grooming salon after all.

COUNCILLOR DRAKE "Doggy Style"...

TRISHA Hmmmmm, "Doggy Style"

COUNCILLOR DRAKE "Doggy Style"...interesting...very interesting...

PHOTOGRAPHER *(shouting)* And one last time ladies... SMILE!

They all smile, flashlight from the camera.

TRISHA Alright girls. Showtime over. Time to get ready for the game.

The girls all rush centre stage and place their hand in the circle shouting 'Terriers' as they raise their fists.

Music **"WHO LET THE DOGS OUT"** *loudly fills the stage as they all exit singing along and enjoying the moment.* **ASBO** *collects the* **COUNCILLOR** *and dances off with him.*

Whistle blows.

Blackout.

End of Act One – Interval

ACT II

Scene One

The netball game directly after the photo shoot that ends Act I.

Lighting is focused on the subs benches and the spotlit "frozen" balletic moments on the netball pitch as the script dictates.

In the darkness we hear TRISHA's *voice as at the end of Act I.*

TRISHA'S VOICE Alright girls. Showtime over. Time to get ready for the game.

A whistle blows in the darkness.

The lights snap up on the subs bench. Trisha is stood on the bench addressing the team who are gathered around her. Some of the girls are warming up as she talks. Loud motivational music is blaring out that will end when the whistle blows for the start of the game. Some of the girls are adjusting/tightening their high pony tails. The players' bags/jackets/trackie bottoms and water bottles are piled up round the bench. The two subs JACKIE *and* ANGIE *are slightly detached from the group and are passing a netball back and forth to each other and having a shot at the net while the team talk takes place.*

TRISHA I want you all to enjoy yourselves tonight. Try not to tense up too much. Think about the things we discussed at the last training session. Defence – stay with your players, attack – "go for all of your shots" – communicate – and stay composed.

We hear a shout of "thirty seconds. Thirty seconds" from the referee. The blaring music fades out quickly. The girls react to the refs shout by putting down water bottles and coming together very quickly into a circle round the coach, arms round each other's shoulders.

Remember girls – actions speak louder than coaches.

ANNA This is your captain speaking – LET'S DO THIS!

ALL LET'S DO IT!

High fives and whoops and off the team go on to the pitch leaving the two subs ANGIE *and* JACKIE, *and the coach* TRISHA, *at the bench. The pitch is in semi-darkness and the subs bench is brightly lit. A lot of noise, ie shouts of players/spectators can be heard.*

TRISHA Keep your eye on the time Jackie.

JACKIE Will do boss. Fifteen minutes a quarter. *(Checking her watch)*

The girls assume their positions. Momentary pause as they wait for the whistle. The whistle blows. The bench is spotlit and the action on the netball court is dimly lit as the netballers go through a series of surreal representational moves – modern dance for netball! – to the sound of a heartbeat.

ANGIE *(shouting)* Come on! Stay with them.

TRISHA Their goal attack must be over six foot tall. *(Shouts)* Come on Anna, keep her off. Well done.

JACKIE *(shouting)* Watch the middle, watch the middle.

TRISHA *(muttering to herself)* Come on girls, talk to each other...

ANGIE *(shouting)* Loose ball.

JACKIE Claim it Sarah – well done...

TRISHA *(shouting)* You're bunching, stop bunching – use your channels.

JACKIE Get it down the pitch...

ANGIE Good snatch ASBO...

TRISHA *(quietly)* Concentrate...concentrate...

Light on the subs bench snaps off and the background noise does too. Silence, a spotlight snaps up on ASBO *frozen in the moment just about to take a shot at the net. She hesitates and rubs her stomach for a moment and then takes the shot and misses. Lights snap off on the court and the light on the bench snaps on and the sound of a heartbeat. We hear muted groans from the bench.*

TRISHA *(shouts)* Never mind ASBO. Good try, good try...keep it going...keep it going...

JACKIE *(to* ANGIE*)* She doesn't look too good to me.

ANGIE It's early days – we've got plenty of time to pull that back.

JACKIE No, I mean...

She is interrupted by TRISHA.

TRISHA *(shouting)* Short ball, short ball...well played Micky – to Kath – to Kath.

JACKIE and ANGIE *(shouting)* Great pass Micky.

Spot snaps up on KATH *frozen in the moment about to take a shot. Silence. Spot snaps back to the bench. They all cheer.*

TRISHA Great shot Kath.

ANGIE Come on girls – come on...

We hear the whistle sound for the end of the first quarter of the game.

REFEREE'S VOICE TIME!

Lights snap back up on the subs bench and the team congregate there and pick up their water bottles and towels. Some wipe their sweat off onto their dresses.

TRISHA Gather round girls. We've only got three minutes.

JACKIE The score's ten six in their favour.

TRISHA Anna, is there anything you want to say as the team captain?

ANNA (*swigging from her water bottle*) That bloody goal attack of theirs is too tall!

TRISHA Think about that when you're trying to block her shooting. You and Tina stand too near to her when you're trying to block her. Take a step back, remember what we practised in training – that bit of space will help you a lot.

ANNA I think we're working hard, but – listen up everyone – we need to stop bunching together so much.

TRISHA You're right Anna – use those channels girls, don't panic, engage your brain. You're bunching up instead of using the channels – think about what you're doing.

KATH. I feel bad – I've missed loads of chances on goal...

SARAH Don't beat yourself up Kath. Goal attack is one of those sort of positions.

KATH What do you mean?

ASBO Crap or glory. It's all crap or glory in attack.

MICKY Their wing defence is shoving me around like no-one's business.

TINA Well don't just stand here and take it – channel your inner bitch and kick some ass.

ANNA Remember Micky – when you're on that court the gloves are off.

MICKY (*trying to look tough*) Right! I will. I'll kick some ass! (*Back to her normal self*) Hey, have you noticed how clingy these netball dresses are? Do I look alright? It feels a bit tight to me. This material is really making me sweat...

The rest of the team start laughing at her. **ASBO** *detaches herself from the group and looks a bit delicate,* **TRISHA** *follows her.*

ANGIE You all look great so stop fretting!

KATH It's not a fashion show.

JANET You're supposed to sweat Micky.

TRISHA Are you alright ASBO? You don't look too good to me.

We hear the **REFEREE** *shout.*

REFEREE'S VOICE THIRTY SECONDS LADIES. THIRTY
SECONDS.

*The players all hurriedly dump their water bottles and
adjust pony tails etc and dive off back to the pitch. The
lighting focuses on the subs bench again.*

ASBO *(shouting to* **TRISHA***)* I'm fine boss. I'm fine...

TRISHA *(shouting back to* **ASBO***)* Remember – eyes on the prize
ASBO...eyes on the prize...

*The whistle blows for the start of the second quarter.
There is the sound of the general hubbub of the game
with* **TRISHA/JACKIE/ANGIE** *all reacting on the bench,
and a series of fast and frozen spot-lit moments in the
game as follows.*

ANNA *defending the goal – looking up at the six foot goal
attack.*

SARAH *in the centre of the pitch about to pass the ball.*

TRACY *holding the ball high above her head about to
pass the ball back into play.*

JANET *arms wide blocking a pass.*

MICKY *on tip toes stretching forward shouting*

MICKY "Here if you need, here if you need".

KATH *in agony on the floor holding her ankle.*

ASBO *about to take a shot.*

Spotlight snaps back to the bench. Huge cheers as **ASBO**
has scored.

(Shouts) Great shot ASBO.

The whistle blows for half time. REFEREE *shouts.*

REFEREE'S VOICE HALF TIME!

The team congregate round the bench again. KATH *sits down and takes off her trainer and her sock.*

TRISHA *(chucking her an ice pack)* Hold that on your ankle Kath.

JANET *assists* KATH.

JACKIE *(checking her watch. Looks up)* The ref added in the right amount of injury time boss. The scores nineteen fourteen in their favour.

TRISHA It's half time so we've got five minutes.

KATH Thank God.

JANET Let's have a look Kath – it doesn't look too swollen to me.

KATH I think I'll be alright.

ANNA Good girl. Here's your drink.

ANNA *hands* KATH *her water bottle.*

TRISHA Listen up girls.

The girls gather round TRISHA.

Short passes – I want to see more short passes and changes of direction in the second half. Keep possession. They're a physical team so stand your ground. Don't let them push you around so much.

SARAH That Goal Defence of theirs was a bit rough with you wasn't she Kath?

MICKY Where's the referee from?

TINA She's letting their attack get away with murder.

TRISHA Well just quietly shut their goal shooter down then Tina.

TINA Right. I will.

ASBO If their goal keeper puts one more elbow in my face I'll floor her...

TRISHA Hey – that'll do.

ANGIE *kneels down by* KATH.

JANET You alright Kath? Come on. Let's get your trainer back on...

TRISHA *pulls* ASBO *to one side.*

TRISHA Are you sure you're fit to continue ASBO – you looked positively green at one stage. What's the matter?

ASBO Tummy bug. I thought I was going to throw up in the first quarter but I'm ok now... I'll be ok.

JACKIE *overhears this conversation. As* TRISHA *walks away to check on* KATH, JACKIE *collars* ASBO.

JACKIE You're going to have to get a grip ASBO.

ASBO Not now Jackie.

JACKIE It's not just you the drink's affecting now – it's the team.

ASBO Just give it a rest will you. I'm doing my best!

ASBO *stomps away from Jackie. We hear the referee shout.*

REFEREE'S VOICE   THIRTY SECONDS LADIES. THIRTY SECONDS TO THE THIRD QUARTER.

KATH *gets up and quickly and gingerly walks about. She gives* TRISHA *and* ANNA *the thumbs up that she is ok, and trots off to join the others on the pitch. Sudden blackout. A whistle blows as* ROB *enters the scene blowing his whistle. He stands spotlit amidst the frozen girls on the pitch. He has a football in his hands, and is shouting to his five-a-side veteran players as they finish their training session.*

ROB Alright lads. Thanks for that. Great football session. Hey Bill – better luck next time eh? And Geoff – you're the goalie remember – those hands of yours weren't too clever tonight were they? If you want to come down early next week we'll spend some one-on-one time on it...ok...see you then. Thanks guys. Safe journey home. See you... *(He checks his watch – says to himself)* Wonder how those netballers are getting on...

Blackout as he exits. Lights snap up on the subs bench at the netball match. The game is lit as before and the heartbeat is heard again. It is the last few minutes of the game. They are shouting support from the subs bench.

JACKIE Come on girls, come on.

TRISHA Time check?

JACKIE Five minutes left! And then that's it for the final quarter...game over...

Spotlight on **ASBO** *indicating to the referee that she is sick.*

ASBO *(shouts)* Don't feel too good ref. I need to come off.

She starts to walk off the netball court.

TRISHA *(to* **ANGIE***)* Right, you're on.

ANGIE Me?

TRISHA Needs must. She's sick. Come on...

JACKIE Go on Angie – we're getting hammered.

TRISHA Time to see if all that practise has worked.

JACKIE Yeah – get a few in the net for us!

ANGIE tears off her sweatshirt. ASBO high fives ANGIE, then hands over the goal shooter bib. ASBO sits on the subs bench.

Take a breather ASBO.

ASBO Sorry Trisha, I just don't know what's up with me...

TRISHA *(interrupting)* Later. We'll talk later. Have a drink and get your sweatshirt on.

ASBO *puts on her sweatshirt and has a drink of water.* JACKIE *and* TRISHA *focus on the game, shouting encouragement to the players.*

Concentrate. Make it work with every pass girls.

JACKIE Stay with your players, stay with them *(she looks at her watch and shouts)* Three minutes, three minutes...

TRISHA Short balls remember – come on Sarah.

JACKIE Down the middle, down the middle.

TRISHA Come on Micky, good ball – come on.

JACKIE Dodge her Kath, dodge her.

TRISHA To Angie, come on, come on...

JACKIE Come on Angie, come on...

TRISHA *(quietly)* Concentrate Angie, you can do it.

Suddenly ASBO *is on her feet.*

ASBO *(bellows)* COME ON ANGIE!

Sudden silence and spot on ANGIE *in position and just about to take a shot. She goes to shoot, sudden blackout. Lights snap back to the bench. Huge amount of cheering from* TRISHA *and* JACKIE. ASBO *quietly claps.*

REFEREE'S VOICE TIME! *(Final whistle sounds)*

Lights some up on the whole set. The team approach the bench. All are congratulating ANGIE *on her last-minute goal.*

TRISHA Well done everyone. Well done.

ANNA What's the final score?

SARAH Yeah – what's the score Jackie?

JACKIE Forty six to them and thrity two to us

ANNA Room for improvement – but well done everyone

We hear the opposing team give three cheers for the losing team.

Come on girls – as loud as you can – Hip hip.

ALL Hurray.

ANNA Hip hip.

ALL Hurray.

ANNA Hip hip.

ALL Hurray.

They all clap each other and the opposing team, and then gather round **TRISHA** *and* **ANNA** *for a team talk.*

TRISHA Well done girls. That was a hard game.

ANNA You're right – they were bloody amazons.

TRISHA Lots to talk about at the next coaching session – you'll have learnt a lot from tonight. But you did well.

ANNA You all worked hard, give yourselves a pat on the back.

MICKY Their shooters were incredible.

TINA You're right – once they got possession they really made it count.

KATH You just knew though didn't you – when they came on in the second half – you just knew that they meant bloody business.

SARAH What do you mean?

KATH Well, they all had their hair in those high pony tails didn't they – really tight!

JANET And when a netballer tightens her pony tail you know some shit's going to go down!

They all laugh.

TRISHA Hey, I thought our shooters did ok. You all did. It was your first competitive game remember.

ANNA Trisha's right. And what about our super sub Angie getting that last minute ball in the net?

ANGIE Thanks Anna.

ANNA Anyway – anyone fancy a swift drink? The Three Stags? I'll meet you in the car park in fifteen minutes.

They all quickly gather their stuff together and leave the hall. TRISHA *pulls* ASBO *over to the side for a quiet word as the others are leaving.*

TRISHA Listen. Don't worry about tonight. You did alright.

ASBO Don't patronise me Trisha… I'm not daft!

TRISHA Come a bit earlier to the next training session. We'll have a chat then. OK?

ASBO OK.

TRISHA Good. Now get off and have a laugh with the others. See you next week.

ASBO Thanks. See you next week.

ASBO *leaves. Trisha watches her go and starts gathering her stuff together.*

ROB *enters the hall.*

ROB Hi.

TRISHA Hi.

TRISHA *continues to gather her stuff together.*

ROB How did it go?

TRISHA OK. We lost the game but they worked really hard. Still a lot of work to do on some skills but I'm really proud of them – they kept it together. They've well and truly christened that new kit they've got anyway!

ROB *laughs.*

ROB Aren't you going for a drink with them to celebrate their first league game?

TRISHA No – I'll let them all bond without me. They don't need me there.

ROB Suppose you've got to get home to Livvy anyway.

TRISHA Not tonight. She's got a sleepover at one of her mates.

ROB Oh...right...well... I er... I don't suppose you fancy going for a drink with...

TRISHA *(interrupting)* Yeah. I do.

Beat.

ROB You do?

TRISHA Why don't we meet up at The Oak. It's only five minutes drive from here. What do you drink?

ROB Guinness.

TRISHA I'll get the first round in and save you a seat while you lock up.

> TRISHA *exits.* ROB *watches her go. Just as she is about to leave she goes to the Notice board, and swaps the Netball and Football posters round. She gives* ROB *a cheeky smile and exits. He grins, goes to the board and is just about to swap them back when he changes his mind.*

ROB Leave it – leave it! Think about those lovely blue eyes... AND she's buying you a pint...

He smiles to himself, turns off the hall lights. Blackout.

Scene Two

Lights come up on a lit area for The Three Stags pub. The team carry in a couple of pub tables and some stools. They have gathered for a drink after their first league game. Jolly atmosphere as ANNA *is about to toast her team.*

ANNA Right. Have we all got a drink in our hands?

ALL Yes!

MICKY *bursts in with a cocktail in her hands.*

MICKY Wait for me, wait for me...

JANET What have you got there?

MICKY I've treated myself to a cocktail!

KATH Very nice too.

ANNA Are we all here now?

SARAH ASBO's missing...

TINA She's gone home – said she wasn't feeling too good.

ANGIE She hasn't been well all night really, I think she must have a tummy bug.

JACKIE A tummy bug? Is that what you call it?

Lights fade on The Three Stages and come up on The Oak where TRISHA *is sat with a glass of wine in her hand. There is a glass of Guinness on the table. She checks her watch and smooths her hair.* ROB *enters.*

ROB Hi.

TRISHA You've made it then.

ROB Course I have. Thanks for the invite *(he raises his glass)* and the Guinness.

TRISHA You're welcome. Cheers.

They clink glasses and have a drink.

ROB Cheers.

Lights cross-fade back to The Three Stags.

JACKIE Well is no-one going to mention the elephant in the room then?

ANNA Not until after I've made a toast Jackie... Right everyone. Raise your glasses girls. To Trisha's Terriers, a great first league game, and future success.

ALL To future success!

They all have a drink.

MICKY What elephant in the room? What's Jackie talking about?

They all look at **JACKIE**.

ANNA Come on then Jackie. You've been bursting to say something since we got here so spit it out.

JACKIE I'm talking about ASBO... Oh come on everyone...we ALL know what was up with her tonight!

MICKY She had a tummy bug didn't she?

JACKIE She had a bloody hangover – that's what she had!

TINA So she had a few too many to drink yesterday – it can happen to anyone.

SARAH Hmmmm...not so sure it was just yesterday...

JANET I know what you mean.

KATH And she chews that gum all the time.

Pause while they all have a drink and think about the situation.

MICKY Well you can't criticise the girl for wanting to have fresh breath.

JACKIE Don't be so bloody naïve Micky.

MICKY What? What are you all getting at?

ANNA Are you saying she's got a drink problem Jackie?

JACKIE Yes, I am.

TINA A serious one?

JACKIE I think it's got worse.

SARAH So do I. She reeks of alcohol sometimes in training.

KATH She must have the constitution of an ox.

JANET Yeah – she must have to be able to drink like she does and still do all that running around...

KATH I don't know how she manages to play as well as she does...

The others murmur their agreement. MICKY *interrupts.*

MICKY Ooooooh – so THAT'S why she chews gum all the time...

They all groan at MICKY *as the lights cross-fade to The Oak where* TRISHA *and* ROB *are still chatting.*

TRISHA Your round next time.

ROB Next time? Are we going to make this a regular thing then?

TRISHA Oh, I don't know about regular...

Beat.

ROB I do.

TRISHA Oh do you now?

ROB Yeah , I do – I'd like it to be a regular thing... I mean... I like you... I like you a lot Trisha.

TRISHA Hold your horses...you've only asked me out for a drink...

Beat.

ROB Actually, you sort of asked me.

They both have a swig of their drinks and weigh each other up.

TRISHA I did didn't I.

ROB You did...

They both take another swig of their drinks.

TRISHA I don't usually ask guys out...

ROB *interrupts.*

ROB I know.

Beat.

TRISHA I hope that you don't think that I'm the sort of girl who...

ROB *interrupts again.*

ROB I don't.

They both have another swig of their drinks.

TRISHA Good.

The lights cross fade to The Three Stags.

JANET Well what are we going to do about it?

KATH I wonder if we should tell Trisha?

ANGIE I think she knows already.

SARAH She probably didn't pull ASBO off because it was our first match.

TINA I don't think she'll be that kind to her in future.

JACKIE I should think not! It cost us the bloody game!

TINA What do you think we should do Anna?

ANNA I'll have to think about it.

JANET It's a delicate situation.

SARAH I think we do need to tread very carefully...

Pause as they all think.

MICKY I know. I'll take her to Alcoholics Anonymous.

ANNA Very diplomatic Micky!

JACKIE *(hopefully)* Perhaps we should drop her from the team?

ANNA No! Look, just leave it with me. I'll have a quiet word with Trisha.

SARAH I'm more bothered about why ASBO's drinking so much.

TINA Same here.

JACKIE But she's letting herself down...and the team!

ANNA I'll drop her a text before the next training session. Just to make sure she's coming. We don't want to lose her do we?

ALL *(except JACKIE)* NO!

They all look at JACKIE.

JACKIE Suppose not...

ANNA Anyway. Home time for me I think. I'll sleep well tonight. Coming Tina?

TINA No way. I'm getting bladdered! Who's for another?

The others cheer in agreement except ANGIE.

ANGIE If you're going now you couldn't drop me off could you Anna? I'm knackered!

ANNA Course I can. Come on then.

ANNA and ANGIE exit shouting goodbye to the rest of the girls.

TINA Come on girls – get it down your necks. Make room for another...

The girls finish their drinks as the lights cross fade to The Oak again.

ROB Do you want another?

TRISHA No thanks, I'm driving.

ROB So am I.

Pause as they both toy with their glasses.

TRISHA We...we could...we could always have another drink at my house...if you like...like I said... I've got the house to meself tonight so...

ROB *gets up eagerly.*

ROB Yeah, alright...yeah...that'd be great.

TRISHA *is a bit flustered as she gathers her bag together and gabbles the next sentence.*

TRISHA OK then. It's not that far, you won't get lost – if you follow my car... I'll just drive slower than usual and...

ROB *very gently gives her a kiss to shut her up. She gently pushes him back.*

I don't normally snog in public.

ROB Neither do I...

He goes to turn away from her and changes his mind.

Ah bugger it...

He turns and kisses her again. **TRISHA** *drops her bag as she kisses him back and the lights dim and they and the netballers exit the scene.*

A spotlight suddenly snaps up on **ASBO**. *She has her dressing gown on, and a bottle of vodka in her hand. She silently slugs back a shot, and then takes a swig from the bottle. She breaks down. The spot snaps off.*

Scene Three

The sports hall. Lights come up on ANGIE *practising her shooting skills.* ANNA *enters.*

ANNA Hi Angie.

ANGIE Hi.

ANNA Have you seen Trisha around?

ANGIE Not yet, but she usually gets here around the same time I do.

ANNA Right...you couldn't do me a big favour when she gets here could you?

ANGIE What's that?

ANNA Make yourself scarce for a bit. I need to talk to her in private about...you know...

ANGIE Is it about...?

ANNA Yeah...

ANGIE You couldn't do something for me could you?

ANNA Go on then...

ANGIE Don't drop ASBO from the team. I wouldn't want to take her place. She'll be gutted if she's dropped.

ANNA I know.

ANGIE I'm happy to be a sub for now. She just needs a bit of support.

ANNA And she's going to get it if I have anything to do with it.

TRISHA *enters.*

TRISHA Hi.

ANNA Hi Trisha.

ANNA *pointedly looks at* ANGIE *and then the exit...*

ANGIE (*finally twigs*) Oh yeah... OK...yeah... So... See you later girls... I'll be back at the start of the training session.

ANGIE *quickly exits.*

TRISHA Diplomatic exit!

ANNA She's a good kid.

TRISHA Let's get down to business then. We haven't got a lot of time before the others get here. What's up with ASBO?

ANNA Don't know how to put this really...but...well...the truth is that she's had a bit of a drink problem since she came back home.

TRISHA Came back home from where?

ANNA The army.

TRISHA The army?

ANNA She was a regular. Ten years.

TRISHA And?

ANNA I think she saw a lot of shit when she was on active service and she's bottled it all up since then.

TRISHA How do you know all this?

ANNA This is a small place Trisha. Everyone knows someone who knows someone else or they went to the same school. She was a bit of a party animal when she came home...hit every pub in town big style when she was demobbed – and she got barred from a couple of clubs. Even got arrested for fighting a few times...

TRISHA Really? Hasn't she had any counselling? Didn't the army provide that for her?

ANNA She's stubborn.

TRISHA I've noticed!

ANNA People have encouraged her to go – her family have been really worried about her, I know that much. But she won't go. She thinks it's all a load of mumbo jumbo and that she's strong enough to cope on her own...

TRISHA You've got to want to go though Anna. You can't force it on someone.

ANNA I know.

TRISHA I've asked her to come down early tonight. She'll be here any minute.

ANNA Can't you talk to her about it Trisha? She's got such a lot of respect for you and I think she'll listen to...

ANNA *is cut short by* ASBO *suddenly entering the hall.*

ASBO Hi.

ANNA and TRISHA Hiya.

TRISHA Thanks for coming down a bit early.

ASBO No problem.

ANNA How are you feeling?

ASBO OK. My stomachs a lot better now.

ANNA Good.

ASBO Look, I know I let the squad down last week...

TRISHA You didn't let anyone down.

ASBO I did...you know I did...and I feel bad about it... *(She is near to tears)*

ANNA Hey, are you alright?

ANNA *goes to put her arm round* ASBO's *shoulders.* ASBO *shrugs her off.*

ASBO Don't Anna. Don't be nice to me. You'll start me off...

Pause.

TRISHA We just wanted to see you for a chat before the others get here.

ASBO About what?

Beat. ANNA *and* TRISHA *exchange glances.*

ANNA The thing is...we've been a bit worried about you.

ASBO Worried about me?

ANNA Look, I know you've got some issues around...

ASBO Issues? What do you mean "issues"?

ANNA Since you got back home... I know it's been hard for you to...

ASBO What are you talking about?

ANNA I'm just concerned about...

ASBO *(interrupting)* What have you been telling her? *(Points at* **TRISHA***)*

ANNA We just had a chat about the last game, you seemed to have an issue with...

ASBO Get to the frigging point Anna, and stop bleating on about "issues"! I haven't got any bloody "issues".

TRISHA Well I think you have.

Beat. **ASBO** *stares hard at* **TRISHA**.

ASBO Like what?

TRISHA Like you probably drink too much for your own good, and definitely too much for a sportswoman who wants to win...

ASBO Hold on a minute. Hold on! Who the bloody hell do you think you are Trisha? If I want your opinion off the netball court I'll ask for it.

ANNA Hey, she's just trying to give you some advice...

ASBO Shut it you! Bitching about me behind my back... some frigging team captain you've turned out to be! And you *(looks at* **TRISH***)* – what do you know about me? You don't know me – not really. Who the hell do think you are preaching to me about drinking? If I want a bloody drink I'll have one... I'll drink the whole town dry if I bloody well feel like it! But it doesn't mean that I've got "issues" – OK? *(Shouts)* OK?

Stand off. **ASBO** *turns abruptly to leave but is stopped in her tracks by* **TRISHA***'s voice.*

TRISHA Sometimes people need help to get them through the bad times. I know I did when my husband died. I needed someone to talk to – someone professionally trained – a counsellor. It really helped me a lot, and my daughter.

Beat.

Why don't you let me put you in touch with the counsellor that I had. He was brilliant. It was the best thing I could have done for me and Livvy after her dad died...

Beat.

ANNA We really want you to stay in the squad ASBO. You're such a good player.

TRISHA And you're the most competitive – it rubs off on the others. That's a great thing for a team.

ASBO *turns to face* TRISHA *and* ANNA. *Long pause. Then* ASBO *explodes.*

ASBO Oh fuck off! The pair of you. Fuck off will you!

She runs out.

ANNA I'll go after her...

She goes to run after ASBO *but* TRISHA *stops her.*

TRISHA No! Leave it...let her go...you need to give her some time to think about it.

ANNA The others will be here soon. What are we going to tell them?

TRISHA Nothing. Don't mention it. Business as usual eh? Anyway...time to cart all the kit in from my car.

ANNA *nods.*

(*handing* ANNA *her car keys*) Do me a favour Anna. Can you make a start on fetching the stuff in? Here's me car keys. I just need to make a quick call.

ANNA *takes the keys and shoots off.* TRISHA *watches her go then dials a number.*

Hi. It's Trisha. The counsellor's name is Mike Price. I'll text you his number and address... And listen...we're all rooting for you – every one of us – remember that. Look after yourself ASBO. Look after yourself.

TRISHA *hangs up. The lights dim on the scene.*

Scene Four

The sports hall. All the girls except ASBO *are in the sports hall wearing their team strip for their second league game.* TRISHA *is addressing the team.*

TRISHA Right then. I'm counting on you to give Angie all the support she'll need in this league game. Don't let her get pushed around too much, and feed her that ball as much as you can. Kath, a lot of running around for you tonight but you're a star – we're relying on you a lot I know...

KATH I'll be fine Trisha. Don't worry. *(Puts her arm round* ANGIE*)* We'll be great together won't we Angie?

ANGIE Can't wait to get out there.

SARAH You're getting stronger all the time girl.

TRISHA If you start feeling a bit tired just let me know.

ANGIE I will.

TRISHA Anyway ladies. Time for a few stretches before the game starts. Come on then...

TRISHA leads the girls into some stretching. MICKY *talks to* JANET *as they do the exercises.*

MICKY How are you getting on with our Shelley then?

JANET Sorry?

MICKY Me cousin Shelley? Didn't you go to the pictures with her last week?

JANET Your cousin?

MICKY Well, I say me cousin – but she's really me second cousin...or is it third? God...me mum's side of the family's so big I get confused – they're everywhere, like the bloody mafia! She's me Aunty Phylis's girl, well – I say aunty but we call everyone we're related to aunty – think really I've only got three...real aunties I mean...the rest of them are honorary aunties I suppose... Anyway... I'm made up about you and our Shelley! She's great isn't she? Love her to bits

– I've had some great nights out with her and the clan... I'm really glad she's found someone and...

TRISHA *interrupts by shouting over.*

TRISHA Less gasbagging and more stretching Micky...

MICKY OK, OK...

She smiles at JANET *and resumes stretching.* KATH *has a quiet word in* JANET's *ear.*

KATH Don't suppose you're going to have to worry about how you're going to tell the team now are you?

JANET No. Don't suppose I am...

They carry on stretching. TRISH *brings the exercises to a close.*

TRISHA And relax...

They all relax.

Listen up everyone. Remember all the stuff we talked about in training. I'm hoping for a better result this game. This lot aren't as fierce as the first team you played – their scoring record isn't that great and Kath and Angie are two ace goal scorers so let's make the most of it. OK?

ALL OK.

TRISHA Communicate – and stay composed.

We hear a shout of "thirty seconds. Thirty seconds" from the referee. The girls react by coming together very quickly into a circle round the coach, arms round each other's shoulders.

ANNA This is your captain speaking – LET'S DO THIS!

ALL LET'S DO IT!

High fives and whoops and off the team go on to the pitch leaving TRISHA *and* JACKIE *on the bench. The pitch is in semi darkness and the subs bench is brightly lit.*

TRISHA Keep your eye on the time Jackie

JACKIE Will do boss *(Checking her watch)*

The girls assume their positions. Momentary pause as they wait for the whistle. The whistle blows.

JACKIE *(shouting)* Come on! Stay with them.

TRISHA *(shouts)* Come on girls. Keep it tight.

JACKIE *(shouting)* Watch the middle, watch the middle.

TRISHA Come on, talk to each other...

JACKIE Claim it Sarah – well done...

TRISHA *(shouting)* Use your channels.

JACKIE Get it down the pitch... Good snatch Kath.

TRISHA *(quietly)* Concentrate...concentrate...

Light on the subs bench snaps off and the background noise does too. Silence, a spotlight snaps up on KATH *frozen in the moment just about to take a shot at the net. Lights snap off on the court and the light on the bench snaps on.* TRISHA *and* JACKIE *are clapping.*

(Shouts) Yay. Well done Kath...keep it going everyone...keep it going...

JACKIE We're looking pretty good to me.

TRISHA It's early days – the other side have got plenty of time to pull that back

JACKIE Hey Trisha. Do you think I'll have a chance of getting a...

She is interrupted by TRISHA.

TRISHA *(shouting)* Short ball, short ball... well played Micky – to Angie – to Angie.

JACKIE and **TRISHA** *(shouting)* Great pass Micky.

Spot snaps up on ANGIE *frozen in the moment about to take a shot. Snaps back to the bench. They cheer.*

TRISHA Great shot Angie.

JACKIE Come on girls – come on...

The general hubbub of a game can be heard for a few seconds until we hear the whistle sound for the end of the first quarter of the game.

REFEREE'S VOICE TIME!

Lights snap back up on the subs bench and the team congregate there and pick up their water bottles and towels.

JACKIE The score's ten six in our favour

TRISHA Brilliant. You're all playing brilliantly! How do you feel Angie?

ANGIE *(pumped up)* Great. I feel great!

JACKIE *(ever hopeful)* Not too tired?

ANNA She's not tired are you Angie?

SARAH Course she isn't.

JANET Not a super sub any more are you? You're a full timer now aren't you?

TINA You stick it up em girl...get in there.

They all laugh except JACKIE who silently collects everyone's water bottles.

REFEREE'S VOICE THIRTY SECONDS LADIES. THIRTY SECONDS.

MICKY Come on folks. Let's kick some ass...

The players all charge back on court. The lighting focuses on the subs bench again.

TRISHA *(shouting)* Remember – no bunching and use your channels...

The whistle blows for the start of the second quarter. There is the sound of the general hubbub of the game with TRISHA and JACKIE reacting to a sequence of balletic and frozen spot-lit moments in the game as follows.

SARAH *passing the ball from the centre to* **MICKY**.

MICKY *going to pass the ball to* **KATH**.

KATH *losing the ball to the opposition.*

JANET *defending – arms wide to block a pass.*

ANNA *jumping to intercept.*

TINA *striking a defensive pose to try and stop a goal being scored.*

Spotlight snaps back to the bench.

JACKIE Shit. The opposition have livened up haven't they?

TRISHA *(shouts)* Block it Tina. Block it!

The whistle blows for half time. **REFEREE** *shouts.*

REFEREE'S VOICE HALF TIME!

The team congregate round the bench again grabbing their water bottles/adjusting pony tails etc.

JACKIE *(checking her watch. Looks up)* No added time boss. And the score's fourteen to twelve in their favour.

TRISHA How's your ankle this game Kath?

KATH *(checking it out)* Not swollen so I think it's bearing up ok.

JANET Thank God for that.

ANNA Come on girls. We're in with a chance here. They're not that far ahead.

SARAH How you doing Angie?

ANGIE OK. I'm OK.

MICKY Not too tired?

ANGIE Nah... I'm good...

JACKIE You sure?

ANGIE I'm fine.

JACKIE Really? You don't want to be overdoing...

> **JACKIE** *is interrupted by the* **REFEREE**'s *whistle. The girls all chuck their water bottles at her and rush back on to the netball court.*

REFEREES VOICE THIRTY SECONDS LADIES. THIRTY SECONDS TO THE THIRD QUARTER.

> *Sharp spotlight on* **ROB** *amidst the girls on the pitch blowing his whistle. He has a football in his hands, and is shouting to his five-a-side veteran players as they finish their training session.*

ROB Alright lads. Geoff – lot better tonight in goal so that bit of one-to-one training paid off didn't it? Well done mate. Much better. Dave – get that knee of yours seen to at the doctors. Bit of a crunch tackle from you Bill. He's an animal that lad! Thanks guys. Safe journey home. See you next week... *(He checks his watch – says to himself)* Hope those girls manage a win tonight... I'm on a promise if they do...

> *Blackout. Whistle blows. Referee shouts 'TIME' for the last break before the final quarter of the game. Lights snap up on the subs bench at the netball match. The girls are all gathered round the bench.* **ANGIE** *is sat down with her head in her hands.* **SARAH** *and* **TRISHA** *are knelt alongside her.*

TRISHA Well?

SARAH I don't think she should play the final quarter, she's exhausted.

ANGIE I'll be alright.

SARAH You won't. I'm the medic here remember and I say you're not strong enough to play the final quarter.

ANNA Listen to Sarah will you Angie. You've been a trooper, and we're still in with a shout so stop worrying.

TRISHA Give me your bib.

ANGIE *hands it over.* TRISHA *turns to* JACKIE *who has been silently praying that Angie will not go back on court.*

Right, you're on.

JACKIE Thank you God!

ANNA Come on Jackie. Time to step up to the plate.

JACKIE *grabs the bib off* TRISHA *and puts it on.*

TRISHA Now remember what I told you in training Jackie. You're not a natural shooter so you need to pass to Kath for the final shot. That's your role – act as a feeder for Kath. Got it?

JACKIE Got it!

TRISHA Come on – let's see if we can pull it off folks. Get a few more in the net for us.

TRISHA *indicates to the referee that there is a substitution.* JANET *pulls* KATH *and* MICKY *to one side.*

JANET God almighty. What's she doing putting Jackie on?

KATH No choice I suppose.

JANET Well just make bloody sure she passes the ball to you and doesn't try and have a shot on goal? Try and get it to Kath will you Micky.

MICKY I'll do me best – but I think we should...you know...

JANET What?

MICKY Don't be too hard on her Janet. It's her first game.

REFEREE'S VOICE Thirty seconds ladies. Thirty seconds.

The girls rush back on the pitch. JACKIE *assumes her position on court – some of the girls give her the thumbs up. Lights snap to a spot on the bench.* ANGIE *is putting her sweatshirt on and having a drink of water.*

TRISHA Concentrate. Concentrate.

ANGIE Short balls – come on Sarah.

TRISHA Good ball – come on.

ANGIE Down the middle, down the middle.

TRISHA Come on Tina, good ball – come on.

ANGIE Grab it Anna.

TRISHA To Janet. To Janet.

ANGIE Yeah! Come on Janet. Come on...

TRISHA Good move Sarah.

ANGIE Loose ball. Grab it Sarah.

MICKY To me Sarah. To me...

TRISHA Grab it Micky. Kick some ass.

ANGIE She's got it. She's got it

TRISHA To Kath. Pass it to Kath.

ANGIE To Ka... Oh my God! Jackie's got it.

TRISHA Pass to Kath Jackie. To Kath.

> *Sudden silence and spot on* **JACKIE**. *She is about to pass it to* **KATH** *when a heavenly harp plays and* **JACKIE** *is bathed in a heavenly glow. We hear the voice of* **TRACEY NEVILLE**.

TRACY NEVILLE'S VOICE Jackie Goodwin. What a player. A future England star...

> **JACKIE** *turns as if hypnotised to face the net, and in slow motion goes to shoot.*

> *Light snaps off. We hear the* **REFEREE'S** *voice in the darkness.*

REFEREE'S VOICE TIME! *(Whistle blows)*

> *There is a frozen moment as they all stare at* **JACKIE**. *Then they erupt into a cheer and rush over and carry* **JACKIE** *to the subs bench.*

TRISHA Well done everyone. Well done. A draw. We managed a draw tonight. Fan-bloody-tastic

ANNA Amazing. Amazing.

TINA We've got another super sub here.

We hear the opposing team give three cheers for the losing team.

ANNA Come on girls, as loud as you can – three cheers for the other side and Jackie, Hip hip.

ALL Hurray.

ANNA Hip hip.

ALL Hurray.

ANNA Hip hip.

ALL Hurray.

JACKIE It's like a dream! I can't believe it. I can't believe it.

TRISHA Despite the fact that you **completely** ignored my instructions I'm proud of you Jackie, proud of you. Hey – and before you all rush off, don't forget that Anna's organised a trip to the Thunder League game next week.

ANNA Yeah. I'll drop you all a text tomorrow with all the arrangements.

The others grab their stuff.

TINA Come on girls, time for a drink – what you drinking Jackie? It's on me tonight.

MICKY Have a cocktail Jackie...

JACKIE I think I will...

They all exit in a upbeat mood. **TRISHA** *pulls* **ANNA** *over to one side before she exits.*

TRISHA Don't forget to include ASBO in the group text Anna.

ANNA I won't. I hope she comes to the Thunder League game. But I'm not holding me breath Trisha.

TRISHA Fingers crossed though eh?

ANNA Fingers crossed.

Lights dim on the scene as they exit.

Scene Five

We immediately hear the echoing voice of the DJ
*shouting out in the darkness over the sound system –
and a spotlight snaps up on him.*

DJ Manchester Arena – are you ready to party? Are you ready
for the Netball Super League Semi-Final Showdown!

*Music thumps out for the Thunder League game. The
song is* **"WE WILL ROCK YOU"**, *and lights snap up
on two giant mascots – a teddy and a cat – entering the
set to get the audience clapping along to the beat. They
do a little choreographed dance for the crowd, and get a
couple of Mexican waves going. All of the netball squad
and* **TRISHA** *are sat on benches as though in the crowd
at the Manchester Arena – but* **ASBO** *is missing. They all
have drinks in their hands etc a couple of them hold a
banner with "Manchester Thunder" written on it. One of
them holds a giant hand aloft.*

I said, Manchester Arena, are you ready to party?

The mascots encourage the audience to shout "Yes".

Come on Manchester – you can do better than that! Let's try
it again – Manchester Arena – are you ready to party?

Mascots encourage the crowd to shout "Yes" a lot louder.

Fantastic. And it's time to party soooooo let's hear it for
Hertfordshire Mavericks!

Cheering crowd heard.

And for the home team – Manchester Thunder!

*Much louder cheering – especially from the girls on the
bench.*

DJ *plays* **"LET'S GET READY TO RUMBLE"** *over the
sound system.*

And an extra special welcome for our England coach – Tracy Neville, here tonight with her old team Manchester Thunder...

Loud heavenly music plays and an ethereal glow lights the stage.

ALL *(as in a heavenly chorus)* Tracy Neville!

JACKIE There she is! There she is!

*Loud heavenly music snaps off and **"LET'S GET READY TO RUMBLE"** continues and underscores the chat from the netball girls in the crowd.*

SARAH Have you noticed?

ANGIE Noticed what?

SARAH That the Referees are two blokes!

ANNA Bloody cheek.

JACKIE Yeah. They won't let women Referee men's premier league games but they're quick to get in on the act with women's netball.

MICKY Well, my Geoff's really into the game now. He's been watching it on Sky. He's watching this tonight.

KATH Is he?

JANET I can't imagine a fella watching netball.

MICKY He loves it. I quite often wear my netball kit for him when...you know...

JANET When what?

MICKY When he fancies a bit of...you know...

KATH No.

The squad has not noticed that ASBO has joined them...

TINA She means when he fancies a bit of rumpy pumpy.

KATH AND JANET Really!

MICKY Not all the time – just now and then – It's livened up our sex life no end. He especially loves it when I shout 'Loose ball'!

ASBO Micky! You little tinker you...

THE SQUAD ASBO! You made it.

They all go to give her a hug but we immediately hear a whistle blow so they just drag her into the middle of them to watch the game.

TRISHA And we're off...

The girls all shout the following comments out in quick succession and should be sharply spot-lit for each line.

ASBO Come on Thunder.

TRISHA Good interception.

ANNA Over the top.

ALL oooooooooh.

SARAH Too slow.

TINA Move it.

MICKY She's got space.

ALL Aaaaaaah.

KATH Make it count.

JANET Oh Referee ! Come on...

ANGIE Well marked.

JACKIE Give her the ball.

ALL Come on Thunder.

Loud whistle heard. The mascots re-enter as the DJs voice is heard.

DJ'S VOICE   First quarter over folks. And this is a great match we've got going on here tonight. Really close with Hertfordshire Mavericks just in the lead. Absolutely brilliant ladies and gentlemen, boys and girls. Make some noise for your team in Manchester!

Music blasts out **"I'VE GOT A FEELING THAT TONIGHT'S GONNA BE A GOOD NIGHT"** *and underscores the girls' conversation. The two mascots entertain the crowd.*

ANNA   Close thing.

TRISHA   You can say that again.

ASBO   Too bloody close for my liking.

ANGIE   Makes it more exciting though doesn't it! I think it's great.

TINA   Hey, have you seen the cameras everywhere?

MICKY   *(smoothing her hair)* Where? Where?

JACKIE   Calm down. They won't be pointing them at us.

MICKY   They might! And my Geoff's watching *(She waves over to a camera)* Hello, hello... Yoo hoo... Over here...oh I think they've noticed us...they're pointing the camera this way...

All the girls wave hysterically and pose for the camera.

KATH   That sound technician looked a bit dishy didn't he?

JANET   You're a married woman.

KATH   Spoilsport!

TINA *takes some mini wine bottles out of her bag and hands them round.*

TINA   Does anyone else fancy a bit of pinot grigio?

TRISHA   Don't be waving that wine around Tina. How did you get that past security?

TINA None of your business.

Some of the girls take a bottle – but not ASBO. *A whistle blows.*

TRISHA Here we go ladies. Second quarter...

ASBO Come on Thunder!

ANNA Go Thunder.

DJ'S VOICE Let's make some noise for the Mavericks.

Cheering from the crowd encouraged by the mascots.

And let's make some noise for Manchester Thunder.

Even louder cheering from the crowd encouraged by the mascots who then exit the arena. A whistle blows.

MICKY There's that camera again... Hello Geoff!

KATH *(to the players)* You need to get in front.

JANET Loose ball.

MICKY Hey, that's my line!

ALL Oooooooooooh.

TINA Out of court.

ANGIE Their goalkeeper is wobbling the post when we shoot!

JACKIE Come on.

SARAH Turn it over now.

ALL Booooooooo.

Whistle blows.

ANGIE What's happening?

TRISHA Time out for an injury.

TINA But they're all talking to the coach now.

ANNA Tactical isn't it.

JACKIE What do you mean?

ANNA Feigning injuries so the coaches can do a team talk.

TRISHA I wouldn't go that far Anna...

ANNA Looks like that to me.

ASBO Can we start doing that Trisha?

TRISHA We don't need to do that.

> *Whistle blows. Game on again.*

ASBO Game on. Shift Manchester!

ANNA Make some space.

SARAH Chase the ball.

KATH AND JANET Come on, come on...

TINA Over the top.

JACKIE Give her the ball.

ANGIE Come on Thunder. Come on...

ALL Oh shit!

> *Whistle blows. Tony Christie's **"SWEET MARIE"** plays and underscores the rest of the scene. Lights fade back up very slowly as we hear the DJs voice blaring out at the end of the game. The two mascots are back on the set jollying the crowd along.*

DJS VOICE Put your hands together for both teams everyone. For Manchester Thunder who've put on a great show tonight, and for the victors Hertfordshire Mavericks who now go on to the finals.

> *Half hearted cheer and clapping from our **NETBALLERS**.*

TRISHA Never mind girls – it was a good game.

ANNA You're right.

JANET Good game, wrong result.

MICKY Hey ho. *(Shouts)* Better luck next time Thunder.

JACKIE Just goes to show – even great teams lose sometimes.

KATH It's been a fab night though.

SARAH Brilliant night. Thanks for organising it Anna.

ANGIE I feel like I've learnt loads just from watching them play.

TINA Right – where are we all off to now?

MICKY There's a great cocktail bar ten minutes away.

KATH You and your bloody cocktails!

MICKY Oh come on girls. I checked it out online. It looks brilliant. Who's up for it?

They are all eager to go. TRISHA *hangs back.*

ANNA Are you coming?

TRISHA I would but I've made other plans.

ALL Oh yes?

TRISHA Yes, other plans.

MICKY Well come on then...tell us...

TRISHA What?

TINA Who is he? Who are you meeting?

TRISHA I didn't say that I was...

She gets good naturedly shouted down by the girls.

ANNA We all know. It's Rob isn't it?

MICKY Shush now girls – leave her be now... *(Teasing)* Has he felt your boobies yet Trisha?

TRISHA Oh Christ Micky. Pack it in will you. I am so embarrassed...

ANNA Well don't be.

TINA We're made up for you Trisha.

ANGIE He's a lovely guy.

TRISHA Aah, go on you lot – get lost and have a good time. I'll see you all at training on Thursday night. Go on...bugger off and have a few jars...

All the girls say their goodbyes and leave. TRISHA *turns to clear up the rubbish the girls have left behind. She does not see* ASBO *who has hung back.*

ASBO I got your message... I rang him...the counsellor...

TRISHA Did you?

ASBO Yeah...sorry it's taken me so long to tell you.

Beat.

TRISHA Don't apologise...little steps...that's what it takes ASBO ...little steps like we do in training...

ASBO *nods.*

Beat.

ASBO I'll check out the alcohol-free cocktails...

TRISHA Good idea...

Beat.

Remember ASBO, eyes on the prize...

ASBO Eyes on the prize...yeah...eyes on the prize... I know... I know... I'm gonna give it a go you know... I am...

ASBO *goes to exit but suddenly turns back and hugs* TRISHA.

TRISHA Now go on, off you go. Go and have a good night with the girls.

ASBO *exits.*

TRISHA*'s mobile rings.*

Hello Rob. Yep... I'm on my way... What's that?...Did we win? *(She goes to say "No" but stops herself. A seconds beat. She smiles)* Yeah...yeah... I think we did...we had a big win tonight...a really big win...

TRISHA *hangs up, and looks around the arena with a smile on her face as **"THINGS CAN ONLY GET BETTER"** plays out from the sound system. The lights* *dim slowly to a blackout. Music continues to play. Suddenly* TRISHA *blows her whistle and the lights snap on again. The girls are back on the set in their netball strip. We are back in the sports hall and they expertly complete a fast choreographed mini training session and* **"THINGS CAN ONLY GET BETTER"** *blasts out as the scene and the play end on a triumphal note.*

The End

PROPERTY LIST

Act I – pre-set notice board, netball net, benches, bin

Act I, Scene 1

Vets football Poster	Rob
Netballs / mini hurdles/ discs	
Mobil	
Watch	
Whistle	
Bottle of water	Trisha
Training bags	Kath
Bottles of water	Janet
Rope ladders	Trisha
Training bags etc	
Chewing gum (ASBO)	ASBO. Micky. Tina. Angie. Sarah.Jackie
Training bag	Anna
Tracy Neville image / Angel	
Whistle	Trisha

Act I, Scene 2

Financial papers	Rob
Mobile	Rob

Act I, Scene 3

Football notice	Rob
Netball	Angie
Training bag	Angie
Training bag	Sarah
Netballs	Trisha
Training eqpt as in Scene I	Anna/ASBO
Nail clippers, whistle, chewing gum	Trisha/ASBO
Training bags etc	Kath, Janet, Jackie, Micky, Tina

Act I, Scene 4

Mobile	Rob

Act I, Scene 5

Bottle of vodka	ASBO
Chewing gum	
Training bag	
Training bag	
Sweatshirt	Jackie
Car keys	Sarah

Neville image/ angel
Mobile   Anna
Training bags   Anna and Tina

Act I, Scene 6
Cheque for £160, whistle netball   Trisha
New kit sweatshirts   Anna
Chewing gum   ASBO
Iphone
Camera etc   Photographer

Act II, Scene 1 Sports Hall
Trg Bags. Water bottles, towels, sweatshirts, netball   Squad
    First Aid Bag containing ice packs, stopwatch, watch Trisha/Jackie
Ice Packs   Trisha/Kath
Football   Rob
Watch

Act II, Scene 2 Three Stags pub
Bar chairs/stools x 4, small table, drinks cocktail   Squad

Act II, Scene 3 The Oak pub
Small table, bar chairs x 2, glass of Guinness, glass of wine
                                                   Trisha and
Rob
Handbag Trisha   Trisha

Act II, Scene 4 sports hall
Netball   Angie
Sports Bag   Anna
Car Keys. Sports bag
Trisha
Mobile
Trisha

Act II, Scene 5
Mike   DJ
Decks   DJ
Mascot outfit
Mascot
Manchester thunder
Banner   Jackie
Giant hands   Kath & Janet
Handbags squad
Wine and some plastic glasses   Tina
MobileWhistle   Trisha

SOUND EFFECTS & LIGHTING PLOT FOR 'BOUNCING BACK'

PAGE No	CUE	SOUND FX	LIGHTING PLOT
1	Opening music fades	Background noise of a sports hall – fade out as Rob starts to speak	Fade up on whole set as Rob enters
2	Rob exits	Fade up the sound fx of a sports hall	Whole set
2	Trish setting up the room for the training session	Trisha's mobile phone rings. Fade out sports hall sounds as she speaks	Whole set
10	Jackie: "World cup is coming to Liverpool in 2019"	A heavenly harp plays	Snap spotlight on the bench
10	All. "The Netball World Cup. Ooh"	Harp snaps off	Snaps back to the sports hall
10	Anna: "Was Tracy Neville there? She's amazing"	Heavenly harp plays	Snap spotlight on the bench
10	All: Tracy Neville. Aaaaah. She's an angel	Harp snaps off	Snaps back to the sports hall
10	Jackie: "she's the England Coach now isn't she?"	Harp plays again	Snap spotlight on the bench
10	All: Engerland, Engerland... Engerland *(the netballers all jump up)* ENGERLAND... ENGERLAND...		Snaps back to the sports hall
13	Trisha starts to set up the eqpt for the circuit	BING BONG on loudspeaker and Rob's announcement	Whole set
16	Trisha: ...so find yourself a bit of individual space – and go!	Trisha blows her whistle and does so as the script dicates in the warm up	

16	Circuit. Trisha says "Start on the whistle' and blows her whistle"	Tina blows a short sharp blast on her whistle. Choreographed circuit with music and lights becoming faster and faster with the netballers being frozen in time as lights snap off and on various pieces of equipment	Momentary blackout and the lights snap up on the netballers moving clockwise and faster and faster round the circuit at a manic pace. Full lights then snap on to show them all on the verge of collapse.
18	Rob: "Thank you. Anyway, as I was saying"	Trisha's phone rings	
19	Rob looks at his paperwork after hanging up	Sound fx of sports hall fades up as he leaves – keep sound fx of sports hall going to introduce the next scene	Fade out as Rob leaves
20	Angie enters	Sports hall sound fx	Fade up on sports hall
29	Trisha: You need to think of something you've all got in common	Trisha's phone rings	
31	Trisha blows the whistle		Quick fade to blackout
32	Rob on set. Telephone conversation with his mum		Spotlit scene Fade out as he hangs up the phone
33	ASBO on set		Spotlit scene Fade out at she exits
33	Jackie in her hallway. Spotlit scene	In the blackout we hear the ding dong of a doorbell	Large spot on Jackie's hallway
34	Jackie "Ah. That'd be great wouldn't it?"	Heavenly harp and Tracy Neville's voice as script dictates	Tight spot on Jackie. Back to larger spot as Sarah brings Jackie back to reality

34	Jackie and Tina exit		Spot cross fades to spotlit scene with Kath and Janet
35	Kath and Janet exit		Spot cross fades to spotlit scene with Anna and Tina
35	Tina "I can't wait to see the new kit it on everyone"	Anna's mobile phone rings	
36	Anna and Tina exit		Spot fades out
37	Rob enters	Sports hall sound fx	Lights fade up on Sports Hall
38	Silence as Rob and Trisha look at each other	Sudden loud music "Vogue" by Madonna as ASBO and the others enter	
42	The girls all rush centre stage and place their hand in the circle shouting "Terriers" as they raise their fists	Music "Who let the Dogs Out" loudly fills the stage as they all exit singing along and enjoying the moment.	Lights fade on the scene as ASBO collects the councillor and dances off with him
42		Whistle blows	Blackout

Interval

43		Trisha's voice and the whistle blows in the darkness	Blackout
43	Lights up	Loud motivational music is heard.	Music fades down as Trisha to the team
43	Trisha "stay composed"	Referee shouts "30 seconds. 30 seconds"	Music fades out quickly
44	Netballers take up positions on the netball court. Momentary silence	Whistle blows Then The netballers go through a series of surreal representational moves to the sound of a heartbeat	The bench is spotlit and the action on the netball court is dimly lit

44	Trisha "Concentrate, concentrate…"	Snap off background noise as the lights snap to spotlight on ASBO	Spotlight snaps up on ASBO. She takes the shot and lights snap off on the court and back to the bench
45	ASBO misses	Background noise snaps on again	
45	Jackie and Angie: "Great pass Micky"	Silence	Spot snaps up on Kath about to take a shot. Silence. Spot snaps back to the bench.
45	Angie "Come on, come on"	Whistle sounds for end of quarter. Referee shouts "Time"	Full lights on the subs bench
46	Trisha: "Are you alright ASBO. You don't look so good to me"	Referee shouts "30 seconds ladies, 30 seconds"	
47	Trisha: "Eyes on the prize ASBO. Eyes on the prize"	Whistle blows	
47	Spotlit moments in the game as the script dictates	As script dictates	As script dictates
47	Trisha: "Great shot ASBO"	Whistle blows. Referee shouts "Half time"	Full lights on the bench as the girls gather round
49	ASBO stomps away from Jackie The team take up their positions for the third quarter	Referee's voice: Thirty seconds Ladies…' Whistle blows.	
49	Girls are frozen in time as Rob enters	Rob enters blowing his whistle	Spotlit scene on Rob in the middle of the netballers
49	Rob "Wonder how those netballers are getting on"	Sound of the heartbeat in the game again	Spot on Rob snaps off and spot on bench snaps on. Game dimly lit

50	Jackie: Five minutes left! And then that's it for the final quarter...game over...		Spotlight on ASBO indicating to the referee that she is sick. Then lights back on the bench
51	ASBO: Come on Angie	Spectator noise snaps off. Silence	Spotlight on Angie
51	Angie takes the shot. Huge cheering from the bench	Referee shouts "TIME." Whistle blows	Lights snap back on the bench and then fade up on the whole set
52	Anna: "Well done everyone"	We hear the opposing team giving three cheers	
54	Rob exits	As lights fade out sond fx of a jolly pub fade upt	Fade to blackout
55	Netballers enter	Sound fx of a jolly pub which fades out as they chat	Lights up on Three Stags
55	Jackie: "A tummy bug? Is that what you call it?"	Sound fx of a jolly pub fade out Quiet pub – The Oak	Lights cross fade to The Oak
56	Rob: Cheers	Sound fx of jolly pub fade up	Lights cross fade to Three Stags
57	Micky: "Oooooh – so THAT'S why she chews gum all the time..."	Sound fx of a jolly pub fade out Quiet pub – The Oak	Lights cross fade to The Oak
58	Rob & Trisha have another swig of their drinks	Sound fx of jolly pub fade up	Lights cross fade to Three Stags
	Trisha: "Good"		
59	Tina: "Come on girls – get it down your necks. Make room for another..."	Sound fx of a jolly pub fade out Quiet pub – The Oak	Lights cross fade to The Oak
60	Rob and Trisha kiss	Pub noises fade out slowly	Dim the lights as the netballers and Rob and Trisha exit
60	ASBO alone at home	Silence	Spotlit scene on ASBO Spot fades as she exits

61	Angie enters	Sound fx of sports hall	Lights fade up on sports hall
65	Trisha hangs up	In the darkness we hear the sound of the sports hall	Quick fade
67	Act II Sc Four. The girls are all present except ASBO	Background noise of sports hall that fades out as Trisha speaks to the team	Lights come up on the sports hall for another match
68	Trisha: "Communicate and stay composed"	Referee shouting "Thirty seconds. Thirty seconds"	
68	All shout "Lets do it"		Lighting changes for match sequence. Dimly lit on the court and spot on subs bench
69	Jackie "Will do Boss". Momentary pause then	Whistle blows	
69	Trisha "Concentrate"

Trisha and Jackie are clapping | Silence | Light on the subs bench snaps off. A spotlight snaps up on Kath frozen in the moment just about to take a shot at the net. Lights snap off on the court and the light on the bench snaps on. |
| 69 | Jackie & Trisha "Great pass Micky"

They cheer | Silence | Spot snaps up on Angie frozen in the moment about to take a shot.

Snaps back to the bench. |
| 70 | Jackie"Come on Girls, come on" | Referee's voice "Time" | Lights back up on and around the subs bench and the team congregate there and pick up their water bottles and towels. |

70	Tina "You stick it up 'em girl. Get in there"	Referee's voice "Thirty Seconds. Thirty seconds"	
70	Micky: Come on folks. Let's kick some ass...'		The players all charge back on court. The lighting focuses on the subs bench
70 & 71	Trisha: *(shouting)* "Remember – no bunching and use your channels..."	The whistle blows for the start of the second quarter. There is the sound of the general hubbub of the game	A sequence of balletic and frozen spot-lit moments in the game as follows: Sarah passing the ball from the centre to Micky Micky going to pass the ball to Kath Kath losing the ball to the opposition Janet defending – arms wide to block a pass Anna jumping to intercept Tina striking a defensive pose to try and stop a goal being scored Then Spotlight snaps back to the bench
71	Trisha: "Block it Tina. Block it!"	The whistle blows Referee shouts "HALF TIME!"	Lights on and around the subs bench as the team congregate there

72   Jackie: Really? You   *Jackie is interrupted*
don't want to be   *by a whistle.*
overdoing...   Referee shouts:
        "THIRTY   Sharp spotlight
        SECONDS   on Rob amidst
        LADIES. THIRTY   the girls on the
        SECONDS TO   pitch blowing his
        THE THIRD   whistle.
        QUARTER."

		Whistle blows.	Blackout
72	Rob: "...I'm on a promise if they do..."	Referee shouts "TIME" for the last break before the final quarter of the game.	Lights snap up on the subs bench at the netball match.
73	Micky: "Don't be too hard on her Janet. It's her first game"	Referee's Voice: "Thirty seconds ladies. Thirty seconds"	
73	The girls rush back on the pitch.		*Lights snap to a spot on the bench*
74	Trisha: "Pass to Kath Jackie. To Kath"	Sudden silence and spot on Jackie. She is about to pass it to Kath when a heavenly harp plays and Jackie is bathed in a heavenly glow. We hear the voice of Tracey Neville saying: Jackie Goodwin. "What a player. A future England star..."	Sudden silence and spot on Jackie. She is about to pass it to Kath when a heavenly harp plays and Jackie is bathed in a heavenly glow.
74	Jackie turns as if hypnotised to face the net, and in slow motion goes to shoot	We hear the Referee's voice in the darkness: "TIME!" *(Whistle sounds)*	Lights snaps off. Then Lights snap back up on the whole set.
74	Tina: "We've got another super sub here"	We hear the opposing team give three cheers	
75	Anna: "Fingers crossed"		Lights fade on the scene as Anna and Trisha exit

76	Act II Sc Five Manchester Arena	We immediately hear the echoing voice of a DJ shouting out in the darkness over the sound system	Spotlight snaps up on the DJ and roving lights move on the audience
76 & 77		Crowd noises and songs play as indicated in the script ie "We will rock you" and then "Lets get ready to rumble"	Lights up on the girls sat in front of a giant screen on which images are shown as indicated in the script
77	DJ: And an extra special welcome for our England coach – Tracy Neville – here tonight with her old team Manchester Thunder...	Loud heavenly music plays	An ethereal glow fills the stage
77	Jackie: "There she is , there she is"	Heavenly music snaps off and "LETS GET READY TO RUMBLE" underscores the girls chit chat	Lights snap back to the arena
78	Team "ASBO, You made it!"	Whistle blows. Music stops. Spectator sound fx underscores girls comments	
78	All "Come on Thunder"	Loud whistle DJs voice followed by "I'VE GOTTA FEELING THAT TONIGHTS GONNA BE A GOOD NIGHT" This underscores the girls' conversation	Sharp light on the girls watching the game as the script dictates

80	Anna "Go Thunder"	DJ speaks and crowd nose blares out as indicated in the script. The whistle blows	
80	All: "Booooo"	Whistle blows	
80	Trisha: "We don't need to do that"	Whistle blows	
81	All: "Oh Shit!"	Whistle blows. "SWEET MARIE" blares out and underscores the rest of the scene. DJ's voice blares out as indicated in the script	Full arena lights
83	ASBO exits	Trisha's phone rings	
83	Trisha hangs up and looks round the arena	"THINGS CAN ONLY GET BETTER" plays till the end of the show as indicated in the script for the end routine	Lights quick fade on Trisha and then come back up on the netball team for their triumphant finale

COSTUMES

ACT I

SC 1/SC 2/Sc3/SC 4. Sports hall.

Trisha and the girls wear training kit. Trisha carries a whistle. All carry training gear and eqpt/bags/water bottles. Trisha needs to look more "professional" than the others. Girls wear different colour tops and some jewellery which will be taken off when the coach dictates.

Rob – polo shirt and either shorts or tracky bottoms, has posters for start of Act I.

SC 5. Night of the first game. Girls at home.

Netballers getting ready at home to go to the Sports hall. Training gear and kit.

SC 6. Night of the First game. Sports hall.

Rob. Polo shirt and training gear. Trisha – training gear.

Netballers. Match kit (without sweatshirts on until the script dictates). Water bottles. Towels.

Councillor. Smart dress with a tie in council colours of red and white.

Photographer. Smart casual attire. Carrying cameras.

ACT II

Sc 1. Sports hall.

Girls and Trisha dressed as per Act I Sc 6. Sweatshirts off for those playing. Sweatshirts on for Angie and Jackie. Sweatshirts/water bottles and small hand towels carried on by players and placed round the bench.

Rob – outdoor jacket on over polo shirt, jeans or tracky bottoms and polo shirt. Whistle round neck.

Sc 2. Pub scenes.

Girls – jackets/coats on over netball kit. Handbags for some. Some with glass of wine. Some with bottle of beer. Micky has a cocktail glass. Rob and Trisha dressed as per last scene. Trisha has a tote bag with her.

Sc 3. Sports hall. Angie/Asbo/Anna/Trisha. Training gear. ASBO. Dressing gown. Bottle of vodka.

Sc 4. Sports hall, 2nd match. Girls/Trisha and Rob as per A2 Sc 1

Sc 5. Manchester Arena – girls. Casual night on the the town gear. Trisha casual sports gear. Small bottles of pinot for Tina to hand out to the girls. Others have crisps/sweets/cans of soft drinks. Mascot – brown teddy outfit with Manchester Thunder T Shirt on over it. DJ – jeans/Loud T Shirt/ Baseball cap.

THIS
IS
NOT
THE
END

Milton Keynes UK
Ingram Content Group UK Ltd.
UKHW020621100823
426637UK00011B/412